DUTCH TRADE AND CERAMICS
IN AMERICA
IN THE SEVENTEENTH CENTURY

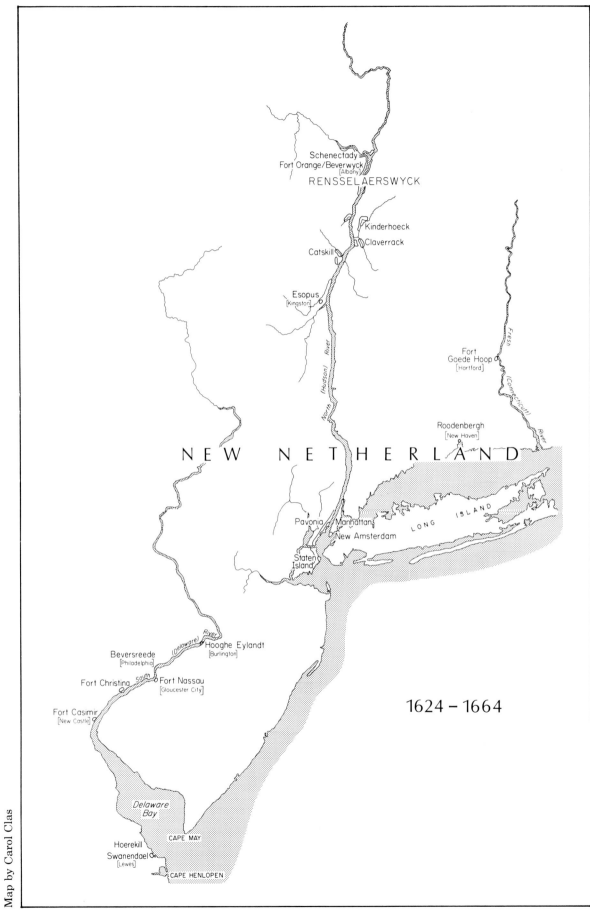

Schenectady
Fort Orange/Beverwyck
[Albany]
RENSSELAERSWYCK

Kinderhoeck
Claverrack
Catskill

Esopus
[Kingston]

Fort
Goede Hoop
[Hartford]

Roodenbergh
[New Haven]

Fresh (Connecticut) *River*

North (Hudson) River

N E W   N E T H E R L A N D

Pavonia Manhattan
New Amsterdam
LONG ISLAND

Staten
Island

1624 – 1664

(Delaware) *River*

Beversreede
[Philadelphia]

Hooghe Eylandt
[Burlington]

South
Fort Christina   Fort Nassau
[Gloucester City]

Fort Casimir
[New Castle]

*Delaware
Bay*

CAPE MAY

Hoerekill
Swanendael
[Lewes]

CAPE HENLOPEN

Map by Carol Clas

DUTCH TRADE AND CERAMICS IN AMERICA IN THE SEVENTEENTH CENTURY

Charlotte Wilcoxen

Albany Institute of History & Art

125 Washington Avenue
Albany, N.Y. 12210
(518) 463-4478

Front Cover:
Woman Plucking a Duck, c. 1655-56
by Nicolaes Maes (1634-1693)
Oil on canvas, 22- x 26 inches
Philadelphia Museum of Art: Given by
Mrs. Gordon A. Hardwick and Mrs. W. Newbold Ely in
memory of Mr. and Mrs. Roland L. Taylor

*Shown in this painting are the four types of ceramics most significant to the
Dutch in the seventeenth century: Majolica, Fayence, Red Utility Ware, and
German Stoneware.*
*On window ledge—Westerwald stoneware Krug; foreground (left to right)—
red-earthenware footed cooking pot; red-earthenware colander; majolica
dish, Wan-li design; red-earthenware ladle; on chest—majolica dish; on
wall rack—German stoneware Krüge; on table in background—Enghalskrug
(wine jug), fayence.*

Back cover:
Detail of cover painting showing Westerwald stoneware *Krug*.

DUTCH TRADE AND CERAMICS IN AMERICA IN THE SEVENTEENTH CENTURY

Dutch Trade and Ceramics is one of a series of research publications of the
Albany Institute of History and Art. The Albany Institute is a museum
dedicated to collecting, preserving, interpreting and promoting
interest in the history, art and culture of Albany and the Upper-Hudson
Valley Region. The museum achieves this mission through its collections,
exhibitions, education programs, library, research projects, publications
and other programs offered to the general public.

Twenty-five hundred copies of this book were printed on Mohawk Superfine 70 lb.
text and 80 lb. cover, and set in schoolbook 10 point.
Typesetting, printing and binding are by Lane Press of Albany.
Design by Thomas Nelson
Edited by Nina Fleishman
Color plates 13, 15, and 16, by Michael Fredericks, Jr.
All other photographs courtesy of owners

Copyright © 1987 by the Albany Institute of History & Art
Library of Congress Catalogue Card Number: 87-71752
    Wilcoxen, Charlotte
    DUTCH TRADE AND CERAMICS IN AMERICA IN THE SEVENTEENTH CENTURY
    Albany, N.Y.: Albany Institute of History & Art
    ISBN: 0-939072-09-2

This publication is made possible with funds from the Women's
Council, Albany Institute of History & Art.

Contents

Preface

In the course of some years of concentrated research on Dutch ceramic artifacts distributed and used in America in the seventeenth century, I learned about the difficulties encountered by those in this country who undertake such a study. The reason for these is twofold: little information about Dutch ceramics is available in English-language publications, and American historians have tended to ignore the early Dutch trade with the American colonies. Since both of these subjects have of late become more pertinent because of increasing interest in the Dutch presence in America during the era of settlement, a book that would at least furnish a measure of guidance for more comprehensive studies seemed indicated.

At first, the intention had been to restrict the text to a discussion of seventeenth-century Dutch ceramics and other wares distributed by the Dutch, but as the writing progressed, the conviction grew that any discussion of Dutch ceramics demanded a complementary account of the Dutch trading activities by which these wares came into America. Thus, chapters about this trade were added.

Although Dutch fayence (delft) has been covered with limited adequacy in books either written originally in English or translated into that language,

this is not true of seventeenth-century Dutch majolica and utility wares. It is hoped that this work will supply a helpful source of information about these, as well as provide useful data heretofore not easily available on Dutch trade in America in the seventeenth century. Since an appreciable portion of this trade was carried on illegally, it was not publicized widely in contemporary documents, yet there remains in both Dutch and English archives, and in former Dutch areas of commerce and settlement, enough documentary and archaeological evidence to establish that the trade was extensive.

As may be apparent, this book has not grown out of academic disciplines, nor has it been written with the academic scholar in mind. Rather, it was undertaken for the purpose of furnishing museum staffs, archaeologists, collectors, and specialized historians with a practical source of information about seventeenth-century Dutch ceramics and the Dutch in seventeenth-century America that has been hitherto unavailable except in Dutch or German publications, or so scattered and fragmented in English-language sources as to require an amount of research prohibitive for the individual. The result is a deliberate dichotomy that may disconcert or offend the academic purist, but, it is hoped, will be of practical use.

Acknowledgments

The writing of a book is rarely the work solely of its author, but is accomplished with the aid of many anonymous persons who give their help generously and with little thought of recognition. I am deeply grateful to all those who have lent me this kind of support.

Dr. Louis Navias of Schenectady, New York, an eminent scientist and industrial ceramist, and Jan Baart, city archaeologist for Amsterdam, Holland, have been my principal mentors in the field of ceramics. The former has helped me to understand the chemical and physical properties of ceramics and the technicalities of firing, with particular reference to porcelain; the latter has graciously taken time from his busy work schedule to answer my questions about early seventeenth-century Dutch majolica and fayence. I wish here to express my gratitude to both.

I owe a particular debt to three people: Dr. Roderic H. Blackburn and Paul R. Huey, both of whom encouraged me to write the book, unselfishly shared with me information and expertise, and patiently bolstered my courage in moments of panic, and Dr. Charles T. Gehring, who took precious time to counsel me with his unique knowledge of New Netherland and the Dutch.

Others who have helped sustain my efforts are Melinda Yates, whose valuable help included translating a foreign-language article and introducing me to new and better methods of research; Dr. Frederick Nachod and my son-in-law, Maarten Spoor, who translated articles from Dutch and German publications; the staff of the McKinney Library of the Albany Institute of History and Art, who gave generous support; Joseph Reeves, former Education Director of the Albany Institute, whose initial support was crucial; Clare Oswald Weber, whose hard work and calm spirit steered the book through publication; Mary Buchan, Mary Dickerman and Ellen Paul Denker, who gave valuable editorial suggestions; Nina Fleishman, whose competent and sensitive editing greatly enhanced the text; and Cathie Gifford, a typist such as authors rarely discover.

Christine Miles, Director of the Albany Institute, Tammis Groft, Chief Curator, and Thomas Nelson, Designer/Coordinator of Exhibits, all have given advice and practical help that have improved the book texturally and aesthetically. I am very grateful for these contributions.

I have particular reason to thank the New York State Library and its dedicated staff for their research support over many years, and the New York State Office of Parks, Recreation and Historic Preservation for cooperation without which the book's value would have been far less. Most especially do I thank the Women's Council of the Albany Institute of History and Art for the material help that made possible the book's publication.

C.W., October 1986

PART I
TRADE

1
Dutch Settlement and Trade
in Seventeenth-Century North America

Although most aspects of America's colonial history have been explored to the point of redundancy, the position of the Dutch in America during its formative years and their contribution to its cultural and economic patterns have been little chronicled. This may be explained in part by the difficulties inherent in dealing with the Dutch language and calligraphy of the original documents and, to a lesser degree, by the unconscious chauvinism of a people whose institutions are basically British.

American historians and archaeologists have tended to assume that any maritime trading done in the seventeenth century with the English colonies in America was carried out by British ships with the blessing of the English government or its subsidiary institutions, and that artifacts found on English colonial sites arrived there in this way. No doubt this conclusion was influenced by the almost superstitious awe with which we have regarded British seventeenth- and eighteenth-century navigation laws. Indeed, it was drilled into our grade-school heads that these laws were held sacred by one and all and remained unchallenged until 1776.

In recent years, research scholars on both sides of the Atlantic, working in a variety of disciplines, have revealed that this was not so. Other peoples traded here in the seventeenth century, much of the time in defiance of English law, and no other so eagerly and with such insouciance as the Dutch. Abundant documentary and archaeological evidence testifies to such trade.

A report of the New Netherland Board of Accounts of 1644 claimed that the Dutch had been exploring and trading along the Atlantic coast of North America since 1598.[1] James W. Bradley, of the Massachusetts Historical Commission, remarks, "The initial pattern of Dutch trade was random cruising along the mid-Atlantic and North Atlantic coasts, the ships of several small rival companies competing with one another." He further points out that Dutch traders "continued to work the southern coast of New England well into the seventeenth century" —and this trade went on for some years after the Dutch had bowed out as a political power in North America.[2]

Because of their almost uncanny talent for trade, the Dutch very early made the Netherlands the leading commercial nation of Europe and became, therefore, the possessors of great domestic wealth. When the Earl of Leicester took Elizabeth's troops to the Netherlands in 1595 as allies of that nation, both he and his army were struck by the material prosperity there. They were equally surprised to see that after twenty years of involvement in a desperate war with Spain, Dutch commerce was thriving, and their consumer goods were not only plentiful but also luxurious in quality. By 1624, the year in which the Dutch built Fort Orange (Albany, New York) to protect their permanent settlement, Dutch manufacture of household goods in general and ceramics in particular was rapidly establishing the Netherlands as a leader in industry.

During this period the Dutch had become masters of the world's maritime commerce. Dutch ships went everywhere, and no harbor was too large nor inlet too small to attract them. John Motley, nineteenth-century historian and admirer of the Dutch, wrote: "Commerce and Holland were simply synonymous terms. Its morsel of territory was but the wharf to which the [Dutch] republic was occasionally moored; its home was in every ocean and all over the world. . . [T]he republic had three times as many ships and sailors as any one nation in the world."[3]

Writing many years after Motley, Aksel E. Christensen declared in his book on Dutch trade in the Baltic, "During the decades immediately before and after 1600 the Dutch were unquestionably the world's leading seafaring nation."[4] England would one day wrest commercial supremacy from this nation of traders, but not until the end of the seventeenth century. For the time, the Dutch were establishing themselves as the greatest traders since the Phoenicians, and over a vastly larger territory.

Until the Dutch West India Company was founded in 1621 and received from the States General a monopoly for trading in the Atlantic, the east coast of North America was open to all. Ships of various nations cruised along it, trading wherever products were presented that offered them a good return. Evidence that Dutch skippers were engaged in this trade before the year 1614 can be found in an official Dutch document in which thirteen Dutch merchants were granted exclusive trade rights for having "discovered and found with . . . five ships . . . during the present year certain New Lands situate . . . between New France and Virginia, the Sea Coast whereof lie between forty and forty-five degrees of Latitude, and now called New Netherland."[5] This claim was in direct response to a resolution of the States General of March 1614, in which that body had offered a limited trading monopoly to persons discovering new "Passages, Havens, Countries and places that have not before now been discovered nor frequented."[6]

The claim of the thirteen merchant-traders to have "discovered" anything new seems specious if one considers that Henry Hudson, in the employ of the Dutch, had explored part, if not all, of these areas in 1609, and that Dutch traders had been sailing along them for some time. Nevertheless, the claim was allowed, possibly because of the influential character of the merchants involved.

Since at first there was no central authority to regulate this early trade, fights often occurred among the crews of the various nationalities engaged in it, sometimes with serious consequences. The advent in 1621 of the Dutch West India Company, with the prestige of its monopoly, discouraged the Dutch free traders, while the growing maritime superiority of the Dutch caused the English to withdraw entirely from the upper Hudson River area where the fur trade was most active. Later the Dutch free-trading fraternity was to renew its attempts to participate in the Atlantic commerce, often successfully, and by the end of the century the English could challenge the Dutch on the seas. For the time, however, trading control was established for the West India Company.

The company's charter gave it not only the privilege of founding settlements but also political control over those settlements, while giving to the inhabitants the right to engage in the coastal trade. Some time later, in 1638, the "Proposed Articles for the Colonization and Trade of New Netherland" conferred on its citizens the right to build "all descriptions of craft, either large or small," with which to "trade along the entire coast."[7]

The twelve-year truce of 1609 between the Dutch and the Spanish had allowed the Dutch to get on with their trade in America and to establish settlements there. The first reference to New Netherland in Dutch records currently available to us in English appears to be that found in a "Resolution of the States General on the Discovery of New Netherland," dated 1614. The area is therein described as

lying "in the Latitude of from forty to forty-five degrees."[8] Originally a private company of merchant-explorers, New Netherland after 1614 would add to its commercial identity a geographical one as well, eventually occupying an area that embraced Manhattan and Staten Islands and the lands north of these, including the Hudson River area beyond Albany; all of Long Island; New Jersey and the Delaware River settlements; and land on the Connecticut River at the site of the present Hartford, Connecticut, usually called at that time Fort *Goed Hoop*.

New Netherland was from the first considered a trading colony, with the dual purpose of exploiting the natural resources of the American wilderness and creating markets for Dutch goods. For most of its existence it was under the direct administration of the Dutch West India Company. Because it was soon discovered that the kind of society attracted to trading activities was not a society dedicated to the hard and sustained labor of providing foodstuffs for a population, in 1629 the company, by a charter entitled "Freedoms and Exemptions," authorized a patroon system for New Netherland. This meant that large agricultural units could be established under the direction and at the expense of private individuals. The charter extended to these proprietors the right to "sail and traffic along the entire coast from Florida to *Terra Neuf* (Newfoundland)."[9] Thus it appears that a considerable Dutch trade with the English colonies along the eastern seaboard was carried on here very early, in part by ships sailing directly from Holland and in part by coastwise crafts belonging to New Netherlanders.

A recent article in *de Halve Maen*, publication of the Holland Society of New York, points out that "examination of . . . source materials relating to New Netherland, reveals the existence of a lively, steady commerce between New Amsterdam and other colonies along the Atlantic seaboard . . . [and this] trading among the various eastern area colonies, though not comparable in volume to the amount of peltry shipped across the Atlantic to the Netherlands was, nevertheless, brisk in traffic and diverse in content."[10] The testimony of a variety of documents of both Dutch and English origin supports this statement.

Conditions at the time made it impossible for the Dutch authorities in New Netherland to police and thus to control adequately this coastal commerce, and many of the traders were engaged in contraband activities. In an opinion given before the Council of New Netherland on July 4, 1647, Pieter Stuyvesant, director general of the province, declared, ". . . we daily experience find, see and observe the frauds, abuses and smuggling which our people as well as those of other nations daily commit [by which] . . . peltries . . . are shipped or sent away . . . to New England, Virginia and other regions, whereby the . . . revenues of our honorable directors are seriously impaired. . . ." The director then called upon "both our own subjects and strangers" to desist from these practices under threat of confiscation and a fine.[11] There is abundant evidence in the documents of the time that his request was ignored.

During this period, exigencies of European politics had their echo in the colonies, and British attitudes toward the Dutch trade there varied mercurially with the changes in diplomatic relations with the Netherlands. Thus, the Treaty of Southampton (September 7, 1625) between the British and the Dutch marked a relaxation of barriers in providing that "the ports shall be open and free for the subjects of both parties as well as merchants" and that Dutch merchant ships could take shelter in English ports without paying duties. It further declared that "there shall be a freedom of Trade and Commerce in the . . . Territories of the Allies. . . ."[12] Yet such trading amnesties could be quickly superseded by the passage of strict navigation laws, or nullified by war.

As early as 1603, Sir Walter Raleigh had pointed out to King James I that Dutch ships, because of their greater carrying capacity and smaller crews, could charge lower freight and thus were driving English ships out of the ocean trade.[13] Raleigh undoubtedly had in mind the Dutch *fluyt* (called "fly-boat" by the English), a craft that contributed vastly to Dutch preeminence on the seas (Fig. 1). This was a unique type of ship with a large carrying capacity which could be operated by a relatively small crew. Parts were designed to be interchangeable and mass-produced—qualities that increased profits by reducing costs.[14]

The depression in English maritime activity and Dutch superiority on the seas continued throughout the first three-quarters of the seventeenth century. By mid-century, English shipping had reached a condition so deplorable that English sailors were taking service with the Dutch. In 1651, by passage of the first Navigation Act, the new Commonwealth government of England took the first step toward rectifying this inequity, yet it would be another forty years before the balance of sea power would shift from Dutch to English hands.

In the first half of the seventeenth century, England was still basically an agricultural nation, and English industrial progress lagged far behind that of the Netherlands and France. English merchants, though a rising segment of the population, were as yet unskilled in the promotion of overseas trade and in the logistics of supplying its needs. It appears

Fig. 1. The *fluit* or *fluyt*, also called "flyboat" (*vliegboot*), was the principal trading ship of the Dutch in the seventeenth century. It is obvious from this engraving that these ships were well armed against an enemy.
Vereeniging Nederlandsch Historisch Scheepvaart Museum, Amsterdam, Holland

Fig. 2. The gaff-rigged *jacht* with leeboards shown here was a type of small craft used by the Dutch in America in the seventeenth century for river and coastal trading.
Vereeniging Nederlandsch Historisch Scheepvaart Museum

probable that the Englishmen in the plantations would have preferred to trade with their own kind rather than with the Dutch, all things being equal, but they found they could get a better exchange and a wider choice of goods from the Dutch traders. The latter had had long practice in entrepreneurial activities and thus were far ahead of the English in ability to coordinate the economic efforts of manufacturers, merchants, and traders so as best to serve marketing needs. Of this, Jan Kupp, who has thoroughly explored Dutch notarial archives that bear on the Dutch trade with the American colonies, says, "In 1665 the governor of the new English colony [New York], Richard Nicolls, freely admitted that it would take some time before English industry could effectively compete in the manufacturing and price of Dutch duffels, weaponry, brandewine, and other goods so much in demand for the fur trade of the North American interior."[15]

Fig. 3. This detail from the early eighteenth-century portrait of Pau de Wandelaer, son of a wealthy Albany merchant, shows a typical Hudson River sloop of that time. In form and gaff rig it is indistinguishable from yachts and sloops used on the Hudson and elsewhere in New Netherland in the seventeenth century. *Albany Institute of History and Art, Albany, New York*

It is unrealistic to suppose that during the first seventy-five years of the seventeenth century England possessed either the material culture or the commercial competence to supply its American colonies with consumer goods adequate to their needs. At this time, a landowning peerage and gentry formed the backbone of the nation, while below these, supporting them, was a population composed primarily of yeoman farmers and agricultural laborers. There was not yet a substantial middle group devoted to luxurious living and equating power with material possessions, such as had existed in Italy, France, and the Low Countries for generations. It was not

until England had wrested supremacy on the seas from the Dutch in the *late* seventeenth century that it was able to generate an industrial momentum equal to producing a powerful body of mercantile citizens. Once such a group existed in England, it quickly developed the expansive inventiveness necessary to achieve an opulent material culture. For mid-seventeenth-century America, however, this was a long way in the future, and the English colonials were forced to rely on the Dutch for many of their consumer goods.

The three Anglo-Dutch wars in the second half of the seventeenth century[16] undoubtedly interfered drastically with the heavy trade between the Dutch and the English colonies in America, but they never stopped it altogether. The minutes of the English Privy Council for August 1662, concerning the "secret trade with the Dutch," charged that the plantations were "delivering tobacco at sea; . . . carrying the same to New England . . . and thence shipping it in Dutch bottoms," and were committing other illegal practices contrary to the Navigation Acts. An order dated "Whitehall, the 24th of June 1663" was dispatched to the governors of New England, Virginia, and Maryland complaining of their complaisance in not preventing Dutch, Spanish, and Venetian ships from trading in their ports.[17] Protests and orders similar to these flowed steadily from British governmental sources throughout the seventeenth century, only to be craftily circumvented by the Dutch trading fraternity and the American colonials. Only one reference has been found to suggest that England ever sent goods to the Dutch in America, even indirectly. This is a complaint of May 7, 1650, by a dissident faction in New Amsterdam attacking Stuyvesant's policies. It charged that "many goods from Holland by way of England and New England come into New Netherland."[18]

New Netherland existed as a politico-economic entity between 1614 and 1674, with a hiatus of the nine years between 1664 and 1673, during which the English held ownership of the area. On August 9, 1673, during the Third Anglo-Dutch War, the Dutch once again took over this territory in a coup, but in the autumn of 1674 they returned it to England by the Treaty of Westminster, in return for confirmation of the Dutch claim to Surinam.[19]

Throughout these New Netherland years and after, a considerable Dutch trade with the English colonies was carried on by West India Company ships, as well as by free-trading vessels sailing directly from Holland and coastwise craft belonging to the people of New Netherland and New York. To understand how pervasive this trade was and what it entailed, it is necessary to look closely into Dutch trade with the individual colonies.[20]

1. Edmund B. O'Callaghan, *Documents Relative to the Colonial History of the State of New York* (Albany: Weed, Parsons and Co., 1853-1858), 1:149.
2. James W. Bradley, "Blue Crystals and Other Trinkets: Glass Beads from Sixteenth and Early Seventeenth Century New England," in *Proceedings of the 1982 Glass Trade Bead Conference,* Record 16 (Rochester: Rochester Museum and Science Center, 1983), 35.
3. John Lothrop Motley, *History of the United Netherlands* (New York: Harper and Brothers, 1868), 3:545-46.
4. Aksel E. Christensen, *Dutch Trade to the Baltic About 1600* (Copenhagen: Einar Munksgaard, 1941), 17.
5. The ships and their skippers were: *Little Fox* (Jan de With); *Tiger* (Adriaen Block); *Fortune* (Henrick Corstiaenssen); *Nightingale* (Thuys Volckertssen); *Fortuyn* (Cornelis Jacobssen Mey). O'Callaghan, *Colonial History of the State of New York*, 1:11; also, J. Franklin Jameson, ed., *Narratives of New Netherland, 1609-1664* (New York: Charles Scribner's Sons, 1909), 47-48 fn.
6. O'Callaghan, *Colonial History of the State of New York*, 1:5.
7. Ibid., 112.
8. Ibid., 10.
9. Arnold J. F. van Laer, ed. and trans., *Van Rensselaer Bowier Manuscripts* (Albany: University of the State of New York, 1908), 145.
10. (F.W.B.), "Inter-Colony Trading," *de Halve Maen* 55 (Spring 1980): 21.
11. *New York Historical Manuscripts: Dutch,* vol. 4, *Council Minutes, 1638-1649,* ed. Kenneth Scott and Kenn Stryker-Rodda, and trans. Arnold J. F. van Laer (Baltimore: Genealogical Publishing Co., 1974), 383.
12. O'Callaghan, *Colonial History of the State of New York*, 3:13.
13. *Encyclopaedia Britannica*, 11th ed., 24:984d.
14. Information furnished by Charles T. Gehring.
15. Jan Kupp, "Aspects of New York-Dutch Trade under the English, 1670-1674," *New-York Historical Society Quarterly* 58 (1974): 141.
16. Anglo-Dutch wars: First, May 1652 to April 1653; Second, June 1665 to July 1667; Third, March 1672 to February 1674, ending with the Treaty of Westminster. (*Encyclopaedia Britannica,* 11th ed., 8:729-32.)
17. O'Callaghan, *Colonial History of the State of New York*, 3:45.
18. Ibid., 1:374.
19. Ibid., 3:234.
20. The research student concerned with seventeenth-century Dutch trade in America should not overlook a series of authoritative articles on various aspects of this by Jan Kupp, of the University of Victoria (British Columbia), that appeared in *de Halve Maen*, 1975, no. 1; 1981, nos. 1, 2, 3; and in the *New-York Historical Society Quarterly*, 1974, no. 2. Another useful group of articles on Dutch trade is that written by Simon Hart, late archivist of the city of Amsterdam, which was published in *de Halve Maen* in 1971-72.

2
Dutch Trade with Virginia

There is reason to believe, from certain oblique passages in documents from Dutch archives, that Dutch ships were trading with Virginia as early as 1611, perhaps even earlier. In January 1618, the States General of the Netherlands was presented with a petition from Sir Thomas Dale, an Englishman, declaring himself then embarrassed by debt and asking that he be paid seven years' back wages as "Captain of a Company in Your High Mightinesses service."[1] Dale had been a soldier in the service of the Netherlands from about 1588 until 1608 or 1609, when he apparently returned to England, to be dispatched a short time later to Virginia as an administrator.[2] In this connection it is important to note that there exists a Dutch document dated January 20, 1611, which shows that the Dutch government granted Captain Thomas Dale absence *without pay* for the space of three years so that he could be employed by Great Britain in Virginia.[3] Although Sir Rudolph Winwood, British Ambassador to Holland, requested that Dale be allowed his salary for the time he was to be in Virginia, the States General *twice* turned down this request.[4] However, Sir Thomas's petition of January 1618 to the Dutch, in the verbose and somewhat ambiguous style of that time, contains two references that deserve particular attention: First, the petition states that Sir Thomas had "sailed . . . to Virginia . . . to establish a firm market there for the benefit and increase of trade," and a few lines later there is reference to his "promotion of trade [in Virginia]."[5]

The Council of State of the Netherlands immediately "for this once and without forming a precedent" allowed Sir Thomas half the money he had requested because "the petitioner is a resolute, serviceable person, and what he hath effected in Virginia is very remarkable."[6] The Dutch have always been a people with a wholesome respect for money, and rarely do they spend or give it away without believing that they have good reason to do so. Yet, having in 1611 twice turned down Dale's request for absence pay, on January 29, 1618, the States General reversed itself and allowed him half-pay[7] and then,

on February 9, increased this allotment to full pay for the seven years—years during which he had worked for the British as their highest official in Virginia.[8]

There is simply no explanation for this Dutch about-face unless it is accepted that the two passages in Dale's petition referring to his "promotion of trade" and establishment of a "market" were discreet reminders to the Dutch that they owed him for past services in allowing them unchallenged trade in Virginia, and that it is to this that the words "serviceable person" and "what he hath effected in Virginia" in the States General document refer.

The year 1612 is usually seen as the time when Virginia began producing tobacco for commercial export. In the eight years that followed, this product became the colony's most important source of income, to the chagrin of Virginia Company officials, who had envisioned a colony that would produce useful foodstuffs.

Tobacco requires not only a special type of soil but also a large amount of hand labor in its production, and in Virginia's early years it was raised not on great plantations but by small farmers whose only labor supply was indentured servants. In the year 1619, however, the Dutch introduced slavery into Virginia. Though only a small number of slaves were brought in that year, the slave trade was a growing enterprise that presented additional and continuing opportunities for Dutch trade contacts with the Virginians.

Through ups and downs, this Dutch trade with Virginia was maintained until the end of the seventeenth century, with the high point coming around 1650. At times, the English officials in London were acquiescent in it and even passed laws favorable to it; most of the time, however, the official attitude was one of opposition.

In 1620, the Virginia Company was so annoyed by a royal regulation aimed at "restraint of the Disordered Trading in Tobacco" that it appointed a factor in Middelburg in the Netherlands and prepared to ship the entire tobacco crop to that country in 1621, claiming that its patent gave it freedom to do so.[9]

This was, in a sense, the opening gun of a controversy that was to continue for years between the tobacco planters of Virginia and the government in England—one in which the Dutch were to play a persistent if muted part.

The establishment in 1621 of the Dutch West India Company, with its monopoly on trade, caused concern among the Dutch independent traders who had for some years enjoyed a more or less steady trade with Virginia. In September of that year, the Dutch "Guinea and Virginia Traders" petitioned the States General to be allowed to send ships to Virginia to bring back to Holland cargoes already contracted for before the West India Company's monopoly went into effect. This was granted, provided they brought the cargoes home before June 1622. At the same time, other independent traders were allowed "to proceed to Virginia, within the same deadline."[10] Still other Dutch merchants attempted to circumvent the monopoly given to the Dutch West India Company by sending their ships to Virginia under French commissions.[11]

Gradually, the tobacco industry drove a wedge between the Virginia Company in London and its planters in Virginia. Unhappy with the precedence given by the planters to the cultivation of tobacco over other crops regarded as more valuable to the future of the colony, the company passed a law limiting the amount of tobacco each "head" could plant to one hundred plants a season, with the added directive that only nine leaves were to be allowed to mature on each plant.[12]

This law was not popular in Virginia, already unhappy over the British policy of importing sizable amounts of Spanish tobacco from the West Indies. The Spanish had a hundred-year lead over the Virginians in developing the domestic tobacco plant from its wild varieties, and they had enjoyed an abundant supply of labor, both native American and African. Moreover, the Spanish tobacco was considered "sweeter" than that produced in Virginia and was greatly favored by British users.[13]

The Dutch, on the other hand, apparently had no prejudice against Virginia tobacco as a trade item and avidly sought it, not only for domestic use but also for redistribution to other European countries and to the Ottoman Empire and North Africa.

In January 1622, the governor and council in Virginia dispatched by the ship *George* a letter to the Virginia Company of London, in which they declared themselves to be "sorry that [the ship *Warwicke*] arrived heere soe late that the most of this year's Tobacco was otherwise disposed of before...."[14] There is good reason to suppose that the tobacco had been "disposed of" to a Dutch ship's captain, particularly since in the same letter there is mention of a skipper named Cornelius Johnson [Cornelis Jansen, in Dutch] "of Horne in Hollande, who is soe farr in love with this Country as he intendeth to return hither; within this Twelvemonth..." and who, as the letter further reveals, had promised to procure and bring back to Virginia a master millwright to build windmills for sawing lumber.[15] This passage established lumber as another Virginia product highly acceptable to the Dutch.

It should be remembered that while the Dutch were undoubtedly eager for the trade, the Virginians were equally concerned with maintaining it because the Dutch could and would supply them with a far greater diversity of consumer goods than their own government could through its merchants, and at a more favorable exchange. This is reflected in a letter written to London on January 20, 1623, by the governor and council in Virginia, which states that "... there have and doe come daylie into this lande so many privatt Adventure[r]s equally recommended unto us, as five times ye [tobacco] Cropp of this yeere will not satisfie ... that except we should deny free trade contrarie to ... your order, doe and will take away much of our Tobacco ... [b]ecause many of their commodities as Sacke [sherry], sweete meates and strong Liquors are soe acceptable to the people."[16]

As we have seen, for years the Low Countries had excelled in the manufacture of luxury goods for all of Europe, and their traders were prepared to offer such of these as the American colonies demanded at prices lower than the London merchants could offer. Evidence of this is a letter from Governor Harvey of Virginia, written in 1632 to officials in England, which declared that "our tradinge neighbours the Dutch doe alloe us eighteen peance p. pound [for tobacco]."[17] This was more than the English were then paying.

During its civil war of the 1640s, England was too preoccupied with its domestic trauma to give much time or thought to the affairs of the colonies, and the Dutch trade with Virginia proceeded at a great pace, virtually unimpeded. As Wertenbaker puts it, "The merchantmen of Flushing and Amsterdam pushed their prows into every river and creek in Virginia and Maryland, taking off large quantities of tobacco and giving in return the celebrated manufactured goods of their own country."[18] According to a *New Description of Virginia*, at Christmastime in 1646 there were twelve Dutch ships moored in Virginia waters.[19]

Very soon after coming into power in 1649, the English Commonwealth chose to deal with the Dutch inroads on the overseas economy by passing the harsh Navigation Acts of 1650-1651, which required the colonists to sell only to British markets and to ship their produce only in British bottoms.

As might be expected, these acts provoked howls of complaint from Dutch merchants, forty-seven of whom signed a petition to the States General in which they declared that they had "traded for upwards of twenty years past . . . to Virginia" and had by this trade enabled that colony to improve itself vastly, in spite of which the Parliament of England was now attempting "to exclude us from the trade . . . particularly to the Virginians,"—from whom, the petition relates, these merchants had been getting furs "and considerable tobacco."[20] In requesting that the States General immediately initiate talks with the English government to protest the Navigation Acts, the merchants pointed out, significantly, that the cargoes they had been taking yearly to America had not consisted of gold, silver, or any coin, but of "all sorts of domestic manufactures and other articles for the people inhabiting those places."[21]

It is little wonder, then, that after years of enjoying this inflow of Dutch consumer goods, the Virginia colonists, as we learn from Northington, "indulged in an orgy of smuggling negotiations with the Dutch."[22] A petition dated 1655 in the British Public Record Office states that in Virginia "there [were] usually found . . . divers ships surreptitiously carrying tobacco to foreign parts."[23] The Dutch ambassador to England reported in June 1664 that "one Claes Bret of Graft near Amsterdam, skipper and pilot . . . of the ship *Sterre* having obtained a full load in the Virginias in the name of an English skipper, . . . dispatched her homewards. . . ."[24]

The passage of the Navigation Acts, a challenge to the Dutch, eventually led England into the First Anglo-Dutch War, which lasted from May 1652 to April 1653. In 1660, Charles II ascended to the English throne, and in 1664, while Holland and England were at peace, an English force took New Netherland from its unprepared Dutch officials. The following year the Second Anglo-Dutch War officially began, and this struggle was ended by the Treaty of Breda in 1667 under terms generally favorable to the Dutch. Finally, the Third Anglo-Dutch War was provoked by the English in 1672 and ended in 1674 with the Treaty of Westminster. Characteristically, throughout these disturbances the Dutch continued to trade with Virginia whenever possible.

Jon Kukla develops the theme that there were four political groups in Virginia in the middle years of the seventeenth century (during which time the Dutch trade there probably reached its peak). He says that one of these groups, a politically powerful one led by Argall Yeardley, Charles and Edmund Scarborough, and the Custis and Thoroughgood families, was a strong supporter of the Dutch trade, and he characterizes the group as representing "a merchant-planter interest in continued free trade with the Dutch that was popular with the lesser Virginia planters who lacked . . . the means to export their tobacco in their own vessels."[25] In view of this statement associating the Thoroughgood family with partisanship to the Dutch, it is significant that one of the largest aggregations of Dutch artifactual remains yet found archaeologically in Virginia was recovered from the so-called Chesopean site, believed to have been a part of Adam Thoroughgood's seventeenth-century land holdings.[26] Moreover, Adam Thoroughgood's daughter Sarah married Simon Overzee, a Dutch merchant.[27] Apparently inspired by the promptings of this group of lesser planters, the Virginia General Assembly in 1647 passed several resolutions against trade monopolies, one of which concluded, "Wee must provide for our own safeties and subsistence in Order whereupon wee doe againe publish and declare all Freedom and liberties to them [the Dutch] within the Collony."[28]

One of the most complete and pertinent studies of the Dutch trade in colonial Virginia is that reported in an article by John R. Pagan, the notes at the end of which constitute a valuable body of additional references that testify to the wide scope of Dutch trading operations in Virginia.[29] Another outstanding authority on Dutch trade, Jan Kupp, points out that "when Virginia began growing tobacco in sizable quantities for export, these [Dutch] merchants were quick to take advantage of this new market for European goods."[30] He further calls attention to the important body of information contained in the notarial archives of Amsterdam and of Rotterdam that bears directly on this Dutch trade with Virginia.

As will be seen, this intensive trade with Virginia that the Dutch carried on both directly from Holland and coastwise from New Netherland was duplicated in other of the English colonies. However, because of Virginia's priority of settlement and its pioneering in tobacco culture, combined with its special social and political structures, the trading relationship between the Dutch and the Virginians is more clearly documented than that between the Dutch and any other colony.

1. Edmund B. O'Callaghan, *Documents Relative to the Colonial History of the State of New York* (Albany: Weed, Parsons and Co., 1853-1858), 1:17.
2. *Encyclopaedia Britannica,* 11th ed., 7:763.
3. O'Callaghan, *Colonial History of the State of New York,* 1:2-3.
4. Ibid., 3.
5. Ibid., 18.
6. Ibid., 19.
7. Ibid.
8. Ibid., 21.
9. Vertrees J. Wyckoff, *Tobacco Regulation in Colonial Maryland* (Baltimore: Johns Hopkins Press, 1936), 28.
10. O'Callaghan, *Colonial History of the State of New York,* 1:21, 26.
11. Ibid., 31.
12. Edward D. Neill, *History of the Virginia Company of London* (New York: Burt Franklin, 1968), 282.
13. Wesley Frank Craven, *Dissolution of the Virginia Company* (Gloucester, Mass.: Peter Smith, 1964), 223.
14. Neill, *History of the Virginia Company,* 277.
15. Ibid., 286.
16. Ibid., 371.
17. Thomas J. Wertenbaker, *The Planters of Colonial Virginia* (New York: Russell and Russell, 1958), 68.
18. Ibid., 69.
19. Ibid.
20. O'Callaghan, *Colonial History of the State of New York,* 1:436-37.
21. Ibid.
22. Oscar F. Northington, Jr., "The First Century of Virginia Tobacco" (Thesis, College of William and Mary, 1929).
23. Wertenbaker, *Planters of Colonial Virginia,* 69.
24. O'Callaghan, *Colonial History of the State of New York,* 2:523.
25. Jon Kukla, "Political Institutions in Virginia, 1619-1660" (Thesis, University of Toronto, 1969), 113.
26. These artifacts are now in the collection of the Virginia Center for Archaeological Research at Richmond, Virginia.
27. Julia B. Curtis, "Chinese Ceramics and the Dutch Connection in Early Seventeenth Century Virginia," *Vereniging van vrienden der Aziatische kunst Amsterdam, Mededelingenblad* 15 (February 1985): 10.
28. Kukla, "Political Institutions in Virginia," 113.
29. John R. Pagan, "Dutch Maritime and Commercial Activity in Mid-Seventeenth Century Virginia," *Virginia Magazine of History and Biography* 90 (1982): 485-501. The author learned of this article through Dr. Jon Kukla.
30. Jan Kupp, "Dutch Notarial Acts Relating to the Tobacco Trade in Virginia," *William and Mary Quarterly* 80 (1973): 653. The author was referred to this by Dr. Charles T. Gehring. In the library of the University of Victoria (Victoria, British Columbia, Canada) there are translations of abstracts of records in the archives of Amsterdam and Rotterdam bearing on the Dutch trade with Virginia.

3
Dutch Trade with Maryland

Although Dutch trade with Maryland began later than did that with Virginia (because Maryland was settled later), there is reason to believe, in view of certain differences between the two colonies, that the former was more concentrated. Maryland came into being as a political and geographical entity in 1634, twenty-seven years after the founding of Virginia. Like the latter, it was established by Englishmen and had a plantation society devoted largely to the production of tobacco and so, presumably, had much the same economic pattern as Virginia. In at least one important particular, however, Maryland differed from the latter colony. Founded as a proprietary government, it was not dependent economically or politically on either a monopolistic company or the British government.

In 1632 Charles I conferred to George Calvert, first Lord Baltimore, a charter that gave Maryland, from the beginning, a degree of freedom in its trading affairs that had not existed in Virginia. According to Newton D. Mereness, an authoritative source on Maryland, the Calverts, as Lords Proprietors, enjoyed "almost unlimited territorial and governmental rights."[1] Earlier, Justin Winsor had written of the Maryland charter, "To the Proprietary . . . was also given . . . the right to constitute ports of entry and departure . . . and to levy duties and tolls upon ships and merchandise exported and imported." He pointed out further that the Crown had made an "express covenant" with the proprietor that no "tax or custom be imposed . . . upon any merchandise to be laden or unladen within the province."[2] According to the charter, provincial laws were not required to be submitted to the Crown for approval, and in the event of a dispute concerning clauses in the charter, an interpretation favorable to the proprietor should be made.

The granting of these extraordinary powers to the Calverts shows the extent of favor in which the Stuart king held that family. More pertinent to this study, however, is the *carte blanche* it gave the Calverts to trade where they would. From the founding of Maryland in 1634 until the beheading of Charles I in 1649, events in England conspired to preserve this

right for the Maryland planters. And in view of what is known about the extent of Dutch trade in Virginia under less favorable circumstances, there can be no doubt that when the Dutch found so open a market in Maryland, they took full advantage of it.

Leonard Calvert, Lord Baltimore's brother, established Maryland's first settlement (if we except the earlier settlement by Virginians on Kent Island) at the site of the present St. Mary's City in 1634, and within a short time the production of tobacco was under way. By 1639, that crop had become a medium of commerical exchange for Maryland.[3]

There are fewer documented data on the Dutch trade with Maryland than on that with Virginia, no doubt because the English Parliament and the Lords of Trade had only titular authority over Maryland in the first half of the seventeenth century, and thus there were not the orders in council and letters from the Lords, to say nothing of harried replies from provincial officials, shuttling back and forth across the Atlantic, that there were in the administration of Virginia. Maryland archives, in fact, refer to the Dutch trade rather casually, and usually in connection with a particular incident. It seems likely that the authorities there preferred to give a minimum of publicity to the trade with the Dutch. There are enough documentary references to that trade, however, to suggest that it was a busy one. A letter written in 1635 by a person living in Maryland declared that the planters there could exchange their produce for whatever they might desire "from any other part of the world."[4] The Dutch were waiting in the Chesapeake to pander to these desires.

Evidence that the Marylanders recognized these things and preferred trade with the Dutch is implied in a governmental order of 1643 prohibiting the export of tobacco in foreign bottoms until all English ships had their complement of cargo.[5] Wyckoff points out that in making this directive the governor of Maryland "undoubtedly had in mind the pressure of Dutch competition for freight."[6]

Obviously, the Puritan Commonwealth that came into power in 1649 had no reason to favor the Catholic proprietors of Maryland. And certainly the

Navigation Acts of 1650-1651 brought at least a jolt to the trade with the Dutch. By this time, however, Maryland planters had enjoyed sixteen years of virtually unimpeded trade with the Dutch, during which time they had received literally tons of Dutch goods in return for their furs, lumber, and tobacco.

Unlike Virginia, Maryland was not named in an ordinance passed by the Parliament in 1650 aimed at forcing obedience to the new government of England from the American colonies. It had been named in the first draft of the ordinance but was omitted, though not granted any special exemption, after Lord Baltimore gave assurance that Maryland was not opposed to the new parliamentary government.[7] Most authorities writing about this era suggest that Maryland was not hurt as much by the Navigation Acts of 1650-1651 as were other tobacco-producing areas. Nevertheless, the Parliament was determined to cut off the Dutch trade on the Chesapeake, and Maryland, as a part of the Chesapeake community, was undoubtedly affected, particularly after the passage of the Navigation Act of 1651. One authority writes that in that year "English ships were idle in English harbors . . . [and] British seamen were going into the service of the Dutch."[8] The same writer says further that the illicit trade between Maryland and the Dutch was not entirely abandoned even during the Anglo-Dutch wars in the second half of the seventeenth century.

Items in Maryland's public archives of 1649 support the conclusion that the proprietor could license trade with any country not actually at war with England, though a tax was to be levied on the trade. An accounting with the attorney general for the years 1649 and 1650 shows that he received from Claes Jacobsen and Jacob Derricksen, two Dutch skippers, a substantial sum in duties, part of which monies he immediately disbursed to pay the wages of soldiers of the province.[9] In 1658, this customs tax was set at ten shillings per hogshead of tobacco exported to New Amsterdam (Manhattan) or other of the Dutch plantations.[10]

Apparently the Maryland settlers and the Dutch trading skippers were on such friendly terms that the latter often contracted to make purchases in Holland for the planters. Sometimes this obliging attitude backfired in litigation, as in the case of the aforementioned Jacob Derricksen, from Edam, who was sued in the Maryland courts by Thomas Hatton, secretary to the Lord Proprietor, for not delivering goods he had agreed to procure for Hatton in Holland.[11]

There seems little doubt that however little the Navigation Acts interfered with Maryland's trade with the Dutch, the three Anglo-Dutch wars, which began in 1652, were another matter. Up to this time, Dutch consumer goods appear to have flowed steadily into Maryland through Dutch traders, but this supply apparently slowed to a trickle during the brief periods of peace between the hostilities in the English-Dutch maritime struggles. Once these were over, however, there is evidence that the Dutch reverted to their earlier activities of smuggling. Wyckoff writes that at the end of the seventeenth century, "illicit trading was another problem [for] . . . the tobacco trade. . . . An incentive for smuggling lay in the heavy duties and burdensome regulations [imposed by the English]."[12] There is little doubt that the Dutch took full advantage of this situation.

Meanwhile, the Dutch South River settlers were busily figuring ways to increase their own trade with Maryland. In October 1659 Augustine Heermans undertook a mission to Maryland to protest English pretensions to territory long claimed by the Dutch. After what proved a fairly acrimonious confrontation for the New Netherlanders, Heermans, in the characteristic national spirit of letting nothing stand in the way of trading, arranged for a private conversation with the governor (whom he had found sympathetic) to sound him out about possibilities "of establishing mutual trade and commerce overland between Maryland and Delowar [sic] bay, which I assured him could easily be carried on, as soon as this question of boundaries was terminated. . . ." Rather craftily, Heermans then pointed out to the governor that such a trade would benefit "not only his Province in general, but himself in particular. . . ."[13] That officials of the West India Company in Amsterdam were thinking along these same lines four years later we learn from a report they made on August 10, 1663, to the Burgomasters of Amsterdam on affairs in New Netherland. This report suggested that the tobacco trade with Maryland could be "very conveniently carried on there [in the South River settlements] because the English in Maryland are greatly inclined to such trade . . . ," and the company officials recommended that "such a cargo as is suitable" for the Maryland trade be dispatched at once, "not doubting but the city [Amsterdam] will derive a handsome profit therefrom."[14]

Almost as if it were a sequel to the West India Company's report to the Burgomasters of Amsterdam, a minute of His Majesty's Council for Foreign Plantations, dated December 7, 1663, records that the council had received complaints from British customs officials

of great abuses cõmitted and done aswell by the Inhītants [sic] and Planters on, as by the Masters, mariners, and traders, to Virginia, New England, Maryland, Long Island &c. who under pretence of furnishing some of those plantaçõns & other His M[ts] dominions, doe both by land and water carry and convey greate quantities of tobacco to the Dutch, whose plantaĉons are contiguous, the custome whereof would amount to tenne thousand pounds per annum or upwards, thereby eluding the late Act of Navigaĉon and defrauding His Matie.[15]

Acting on instructions from the council, the Farmers of the Customs drew up a model for a directive "to send to Virginia, New England Maryland Long Island and other His Mats Plantaĉons, where it shalbe necessary for the preventing of selling and conveighing of tobacco or other cômodities to the Dutch and of defrauding His Matie of his customs...."[16]

Throughout much of the seventeenth century, Maryland enjoyed a unique status among the American colonies as a proprietary government in which the Lord Proprietor had the privilege of trading wherever he found most satisfactory and most profitable, providing his chosen traders were at peace with England. Such documentary evidence as exists supports the conclusion that the Dutch, more than any other trading source, were judged able to fulfill these requirements, with the result that Maryland's trade with that nation, year for year, was probably greater than the trade of any other colony with the Dutch.

Notes - Chapter 3

1. *Encyclopaedia Britannica*, 11th ed., 17:831.
2. Justin Winsor, *Narrative and Critical History of America* (New York: AMS Press, 1967), 3:521.
3. Vertrees J. Wyckoff, *Tobacco Regulation in Colonial Maryland* (Baltimore: Johns Hopkins Press, 1936), 50.
4. Ibid., 48.
5. Ibid., 58.
6. Ibid., 54 fn.
7. Bernard C. Steiner, *Maryland under the Commonwealth, 1649-1658*, Johns Hopkins University Studies, series 29, no. 1 (Baltimore: Johns Hopkins Press, 1911), 53-54.
8. Matthew Page Andrews, *Tercentenary History of Maryland* (Chicago: S. J. Clarke Publishing Co., 1925), 1:231.
9. William Hand Browne, ed., *Proceedings of the Council of Maryland, 1636-1667* (Baltimore: Maryland Historical Society, 1885), 302.
10. Ibid., 347.
11. Raphael Semmes, *Captains and Mariners of Early Maryland* (Baltimore: Johns Hopkins Press, 1937), 52-53.
12. Wyckoff, *Tobacco Regulation in Colonial Maryland*, 104.
13. Edmund B. O'Callaghan, *Documents Relative to the Colonial History of the State of New York* (Albany: Weed, Parsons and Co., 1853-1858), 2:98.
14. Ibid., 211.
15. Ibid., 3:47.
16. Ibid., 49.

4
Dutch Trade with New England

Although free trade as an economic tenet did not come naturally to the middle-class Englishman of the seventeenth century, two things made it more acceptable to New Englanders: (1) the recognition that they had not made the sacrifice of removing themselves to a strange and difficult environment only to retain social and economic shackles formerly endured in England and Europe, and (2) the patent inability of English industry to supply them fully with the kind and quantity of goods they had to have for economic survival. The Dutch offered them a way out of this dilemma, and they took it.

Assessing the Dutch trade with the New England colonies is more difficult than determining the facts about the trade with Virginia and Maryland, largely because, unlike in the southern colonies, the early New England settlements (before Massachusetts Bay) were splintered into diverse types of sponsors and settlers under no common authority and having no common goals. Documentary records of many of these settlements were kept poorly in the first place and are difficult to retrieve because no central agency was wholly responsible for their archival preservation. Therefore, to discover the nature and extent of the Dutch trade with these areas, it is often necessary to rely on fragmented data or on inference based on a general knowledge of Dutch trading practices elsewhere, or at times even on knowledge of personalities involved. Nevertheless, the diligent researcher can find convincing documentary material to indicate that the Dutch trade with New England areas was an active one in the early seventeenth century. Justin Winsor wrote that Captain John Mason was in error in stating that the Dutch began to trade on the New England coast about 1621, claiming instead that the Dutch trade there began in 1598.[1]

Within recent years, archaeological activity at the Acadian sites in Maine has produced Dutch ceramic and metallic artifacts.[2] These provide material evidence to support documentary references to Dutch trading along the coastlines of Maine and the Maritime Provinces as early as the sixteenth century, although since much of this trade was in contraband, it was understandably not widely publicized in documents of the time.

The early settlement period in New England encompassed an *olla podrida* of interests and personalities that included adventurers, political and religious refugees, merchants, fur traders, fishermen, and other elements so disparate as to defy analysis by any but the most dedicated student of New England's beginnings. Because this area was from the first fragmented into these diverse groups, its economic and social problems were of a complexity not present in any other American settlement area. Although in 1641 the Reverend John Cotton of the Massachusetts Bay colony drew up a legal code based on laws of the Old Testament, it was rejected in favor of one firmly rooted in English Common Law—a type of code followed by the other New England communities generally, though now and then religious influences infiltrated civil concepts.[3] The Dutch, devout Calvinists though they were, understood that economics and religion made an uneasy mixture, and were experts at keeping separate the affairs of God and Caesar.

In following their traditional policies of trading wherever and with whomever they could, Dutch skippers naturally gravitated to the northeastern coastal area of America as settlements were established there. Here, the Dutch trade involved the same dichotomous groups as in the south: traders from New Netherland, with or without the blessing of the West India Company's authorities there, and skippers and ships employed by independent merchants in Holland, in deliberate circumvention of the West India Company's monopoly on trade with America. Frequently, these trading activities were complicated by English and Dutch quarrels over colonial boundary lines, particularly in the case of Connecticut. Thus, there existed between the Dutch and the New England colonies a kind of love-hate relationship that both acknowledged but which neither side allowed to halt a mutually beneficial commerce, although it was now and then interrupted under somewhat *opéra bouffe* circumstances. The Dutch, though always willing to trade legally or by smuggling as the circumstances dictated, were quick to resent similar tactics in others. When, in May

1642, a party of New Haven colonists attempted to establish a settlement on the Schuylkill opposite Fort Nassau for the purpose of trading with the Indians, the Council of New Netherland took immediate action to expel them.[4]

A problem that dogged New England merchants from the first was a shortage of credit since they were operating on a small amount of capital, which was quickly exhausted by the Indian trade.[5] Weeden, speaking of the Plymouth Company's trading post at Kennebec (Maine), says of the year 1628 or thereabouts, "A great drawback was the price they paid for credit [for trade goods] at Bristol [England]."[6] This failure of the British to furnish credit for their colonies immediately affected New England's fur trade, since the Indians, far from being as naive as was expected of them, were often quite shrewd about trade goods and demanded certain standards.

English merchants had much to learn about the tastes of the indigenous Americans. Documents attest that in the early seventeenth century both the French of Canada and the English in New England recognized the tremendous appeal to the Indians of Dutch trade items, and both made overtures to the Dutch from time to time in an effort to acquire these.[7] Moreover, it was the Dutch who introduced the New Englanders to the commercial possibilities of wampum[8] because of the great appeal it had for the native Americans and who first supplied it to the New England traders.

The troubles in England leading up to civil war, the war itself, and the generally retarded condition of England's industrial progress all combined to hamper New England's commercial activities in the 1640s. An entry in John Winthrop's journal for July 16, 1642, reads: "Two ships arrived [at Boston] from England but brought very few goods, except rigging, etc. for some ships which were building here."[9]

The Dutch profited from the casual commercial policies of the English mercantile world, and in a sense so did the New Englanders, since it was largely the English inability to provide them adequately with consumer necessities that helped spark New England's determination to begin its own manufacturing. This, it may be pointed out, was in contrast to the situation in New Netherland, where consumer goods were plentifully provided to the settlers but where manufacturing was discouraged or forbidden outright. Even such a necessity to the Dutch as brick was for many years after the founding of New Netherland obtainable only from Holland, until brickyards established in New England opened up a supply of brick to the Dutch living on the Hudson.[10]

Money for foreign trade was short in all of New England, a matter which, along with its effect on commerce, was mentioned by John Winthrop in his journal. There was no single golden product (such as tobacco in Virginia and Maryland) that English creditors in Bristol and London would accept in place of money. The fur trade, which it had been hoped would provide this stable credit and was pursued vigorously and successfully by certain individuals, was of its own nature self-destructive. Once the supply of beaver had been exhausted in New England and its contiguous areas, the fur trade there, never as large as that of New Netherland,[11] went into a decline. Unlike the Dutch in New Netherland and the French in Canada, New Englanders could not expand the trade westward as the home supply diminished because the presence of those two neighbors and the topography of the region blocked such expansion.

Two other valuable products that New England merchants might hope to exchange for foreign credit were lumber and fish. Both were in large supply, but to exploit their possibilities required an abundant labor force, special skills, and, above all, capital. The fishing industry was already in the hands of companies working out of Britain, and without ships and capital, New Englanders were at first in no position to compete.

A money shortage for local commerce was also acute. The use of wampum relieved this situation somewhat although it appears that this commodity was never employed as universally for domestic commerce in New England as in New Netherland. To correct the money deficiency in New England, it proved necessary to pass laws establishing barter as a legal solution for the payment of debts. In 1640 the Massachusetts General Court decreed that "all debts, however contracted, could be paid in 'corne, cattle, fish, or other commodities.'" Connecticut passed a similar law a short time later.[12]

Barter was something the Dutch could understand since they had lived with this age-old economic device for years. Indeed, it was this willingness of the Dutch to recognize barter as a natural concomitant of trade that constituted one of their strengths and contributed vastly to their success as world traders. In discussing Dutch trade with Reval (Russia) on the Baltic, Aksel Christensen remarks that it was "in the form of *direct* barter . . . without the introduction of money . . . ," and he notes further that "a more developed stage with direct exchange of goods, but with the value of the parcels of goods expressed in money, still later was common in the remoter Baltic countries . . . into the 17th century." Continuing, Christensen writes of the Dutch system, "In the letters to the factors and commission agents in the Netherlands we may repeatedly come across orders for *direct barter as a subsidiary way out*, if a shipment cannot be sold for money; rather direct exchange of goods than sale on credit it is said."[13] The adoption by the New Englanders of the principle thus gave additional impetus to their relationship with the Dutch.

For some years the growing political and religious unrest of England under the Stuarts had been a considerable factor in the building up of New England's merchant population, since many dissenters, most numerous among England's merchant class, had found a haven there. But the actual outbreak of civil war in the 1640s involved the mother country in an upheaval so vast that, to quote Bailyn, it "snapped the organizing cords of public life"[14] and of trade as well. The former sluggish flow of commodities from England to New England was now reduced to a trickle, and the merchants there were largely left to their own commercial devices. New England merchants responded with a burst of entrepreneurial vigor that from the beginning focused on the expansion of their trading connections into areas far afield, including the Caribbean, the so-called Spanish and Portuguese Wine Islands,[15] Portugal itself, and the slave coast of Africa. As New England's commerce with the foreign world thus burgeoned, the need for ships escalated. A ship-building program was undertaken that was to place New England foremost in that industry for many years to come, but in the meantime, needing bottoms quickly, New England turned to the Dutch for these, thus establishing a still closer commercial bond with the Netherlands.

Documents published in the five volumes comprising the *Register of the Provincial Secretary of New Netherland* for the years 1638-1660 and the *Council Minutes* from 1638 to 1654 (exclusive of three years)[16] present conclusive evidence of the continuity of commercial contacts in these years between the Dutch and the New Englanders. Typical of entries concerning this trade are the following: Willem Kieft, director general of New Netherland at Manhattan, on August 27, 1638, issued a power of attorney to Samuel Maurick [Maverick] at New England, empowering him to collect money there owed by Thomas Farley, John Drake, Robert White, and George Ludlow.[17] On September 3 of the same year, James Oldham, Captain [Philip] Taylor, Maryn Adriaensen, and Hendrick Gerritse Lichthardt testified in Manhattan regarding a sloop owned by "Mr. Captain Teyler" and sold to Jan Schepmoes and Claes de Veringh "that there is no one in New England who has any claim to the aforesaid sloop."[18] The Council of New Netherland, on September 29, 1643, having considered the case of one Jochim Gerritsz Blenck, skipper of an independent Dutch trading vessel, the *Fortuyn*, who had brought a cargo of wine from the Canary Islands to New England and thence had "come hither and anchored at Fort Amsterdam without passport or permission from the honorable directors," held the luckless trader in contempt and fined him 300 guilders.[19]

The foregoing items from seventeenth-century official and private records constitute only a portion of those testifying to the trade between New England and the Dutch. It was a more diversified trade than that of the Dutch with Virginia and Maryland, but the amount of merchandise conveyed was smaller, which in no way diminishes its significance in the history of Dutch trade in America.

Notes - Chapter 4

1. Justin Winsor, *Narrative and Critical History of America* (New York: AMS Press, 1967), 3:193.
2. See the archaeological reports of Norman Barka (Fort La Tour), Alaric and Gretchen Faulkner (Pentagoet), John L. Cotter (St. Croix), and others.
3. William B. Weeden, *Economic and Social History of New England, 1620-1789* (New York: Hillary House Publishers, 1963), 1:78-87.
4. Berthold Fernow, *Documents Relating to the History of the Dutch and Swedish Settlements on the Delaware River* (Albany: Argus Co., 1877), 24.
5. Bernard Bailyn, *The New England Merchants in the Seventeenth Century* (New York: Harper and Row, 1964), 47.
6. Weeden, *Economic and Social History of New England*, 1:95.
7. Edmund B. O'Callaghan, *History of New Netherland* (New York: D. Appleton and Co., 1848), 1:105 fn. 2; also, letter of Isaack de Rasière to the Directors of the Amsterdam Chamber, September 23, 1626, in Arnold J. F. van Laer, ed. and trans., *Documents Relating to New Netherland, 1624-1626* (San Marino, Calif.: Henry E. Huntington Library and Art Gallery, 1924), 171.

8. In this connection, tubular beads around ¼-inch long made of white or dark purple parts of sea shells by the Algonkian Indians of southern New England and Long Island. The Dutch, finding that these were much coveted by other Indians, used them widely in the fur trade and also as a medium of exchange in the domestic economy of New Netherland.

9. John Winthrop, *Journal, 1630-1649*, ed. James K. Hosmer (New York: Charles Scribner's Sons, 1908), 2:69.

10. In a letter written from Manhattan in 1643 to Kiliaen van Rensselaer in Holland, Arent van Curler said, "Your honor will be pleased not to send any more brick for we can purchase them cheaper at the north [in New England] . . . and they are as large again." (Dutch Settlers Society of Albany, *Yearbook* 3 [1927-1928]: 29).

11. Bailyn, *New England Merchants*, 54.

12. Ibid., 48.

13. Aksel E. Christensen, *Dutch Trade to the Baltic About 1600* (Copenhagen: Einar Munksgaard, 1941), 380-82.

14. Bailyn, *New England Merchants*, 45.

15. Canary Islands, Azores, and Madeira.

16. These are a part of the series *New York Historical Manuscripts: Dutch* currently being translated and published under the New York State Library's New Netherland Project.

17. *New York Historical Manuscripts: Dutch,* vol. 1, *Register of the Provincial Secretary of New Netherland, 1638-1642,* ed. Kenneth Scott and Kenn Stryker-Rodda, and trans. Arnold J. F. van Laer (Baltimore: Genealogical Publishing Co., 1974), 53-54.

18. Ibid., 58.

19. *New York Historical Manuscripts: Dutch*, vol. 4, *Council Minutes, 1638-1649*, ed. Kenneth Scott and Kenn Stryker-Rodda, and trans. Arnold J. F. van Laer (Baltimore: Genealogical Publishing Co., 1974), 204.

5
Dutch Trade with the Plymouth Colony

The Plymouth colony, steeped in piety though it may have been, became for a time one of the most successful fur-trading colonies of New England, holding its own with New Netherland. Although E. B. O'Callaghan, a prime authority on the Dutch in America, wrote that the Dutch of New Netherland and the settlers at Plymouth learned of each other "from the natives," and that until 1627 "neither party had, as yet, heard from or met with the other,"[1] this is a statement difficult to credit. The members of the Plymouth religious colony, who had lived in Holland before coming to America, must have had some awareness of the Dutch in America. Furthermore, Isaac Allerton, a leading figure in the affairs of the Plymouth Company, had been made a citizen of Leyden, spoke Dutch fluently, and, as an educated man and entrepreneur in trading, must have known while still in Holland a good deal about Dutch activities in this country.

In any event, on March 9, 1627, the authorities at New Amsterdam dispatched through their secretary, Isaack de Rasière, a letter to Plymouth pointing out that in the past the Dutch and the English had enjoyed friendly contacts in trade and commercial treaties, and adding shrewdly, "and if it so fall out that any goods that comes to our hands from our native countrie, may be serviceable unto you, we shall take our selves bound to help and accomodate you ther with; either for beaver or any other wares or marchandise that you should be pleased to deale for."[2]

In reply to this invitation to trade, the governor and council of Plymouth, after first thanking the Dutch for having given them haven in Holland for so many years, said, "Likewise . . . your friendly tender, and offer to accomodate and help us with any commodities and marchandise you have . . . is to us very acceptable, and we doubt not but in short time we may have profitable commerce and trade together." Undoubtedly the Plymouth people needed the profitable trade goods which the Dutch were willing to furnish them, but at the risk of antagonizing the latter, the governor of Plymouth added a paragraph requesting that the people of New Netherland "would forbear to trade with the natives in this bay, and river of Narragansett and Sowames, which is (as it were) at our doors." Bradford concludes his account of this exchange with: "After this ther was many passages betweene them both by letters and other entercourse; and they had some profitable commerce together for diverce years, till other occasions interrupted the same. . . ."[3]

Apparently the Dutch very soon followed up their offer of trade, and in 1628, Bradford reports, "The Dutch sente againe unto them from their plantation [New Amsterdam], both kind letters and also diverse commodities, as sugar, linen cloth, Holland finer and courser stufes, etc."[4] He says further that De Rasière came in a bark to a spot near Plymouth and that some of the people of that place bought "sundry of his goods; after which . . . they sente often times to the same place, and had entercourse together for diverce years."[5]

Bradford further recounts that the Dutch introduced the people of Plymouth (and indeed of all New England) to the benefits of wampum as a medium of exchange in the Indian trade, saying that "they the Dutch told them [the Plymouth people] how vendable it was at their forte Orania [Fort Orange]. . . ."[6]

Negotiations between the Dutch and the Plymouth colony took on a certain ambivalence, with Bradford on the one hand protesting his desire for trade while at the same time asserting the right of the English to all the areas in America claimed by New Netherland. However, these differences were somewhat mitigated by the Treaty of Southampton (1627), by which British ports were thrown open to Dutch vessels trading with, or out of, New Netherland.[7]

Over the following years citizens of Plymouth moved freely back and forth between that place and New Amsterdam on errands concerned with trade. Weeden, quoting William Bradford, states that the Dutch habitually brought goods to Plymouth, where "tobacco was exchanged for linens and stuffs, until the Virginians furnished it [tobacco] to the Dutch on better terms."[8]

A curious contretemps in connection with the trade between the Dutch and the Plymouth colony was the case of Captain Stone, an affair that grew out of a trading expedition to Manhattan in 1634. According to Bradford's account, a Plymouth trader "sente forth a barke to trade at the Dutch-Plantation [New Amsterdam]; and they mette ther with on[e] Captaine Stone that had lived in Christophers [the island of St. Christopher, in the West Indies]. . . ." In the course of a riotous party, Stone made the Dutch governor, Van Twiller, drunk "so that he could scarce speake a right word" and then urged him to seize the Plymouth bark with its cargo—a suggestion to which Van Twiller agreed. Stone and his followers then went aboard the bark when its master and supercargo were ashore, ordered the crew to weigh anchor, and, as Bradford puts it, they all sailed "away towards Virginia. But diverse of the Dutch sea-men, which had bene often at Plymouth, and kindly entertayned ther, said one to another, Shall we suffer our freinds to be thus abused, and have their goods carried away, before our faces whilst our Gov\[r\] is drunke? They vowed they would never suffer it; and so gott a vessell or 2. and pursued him, and brought him in againe, and delivered them their bark and goods againe."[9]

It would be thought that after this generous action by the Dutch, with its happy ending, the people of Plymouth would be spared any more contact with Captain Stone, but he, obviously given to pressing his luck to extremes, then "came into Massachusetts." A lawsuit was begun against him there but through the mediation of "freinds" was dropped, and "Stone came afterwards to Plimouth and had freindly and civill entertainmente amongst them . . . but revenge boyled in his brest (though concelled). . . ." He subsequently tried to stab the governor of Plymouth, but being somehow thwarted in this, "returned to Virginia in a pinass [pinnace]. . . ."[10] However, the peripatetic Stone was again incautious enough to return north, where he soon incurred the displeasure of the Western Niantic Indians.[11] These, less patient than the Dutch or English had been with his vagaries, "knoct him in the head as he lay in his cabine."[12]

Bradford also tells of the arrival at Plymouth of a Dutch free-trading vessel in the spring of 1636, it having "thought to have traded at the Dutch forte [Fort Amsterdam, at Manhattan] but they would not suffer him. He, having good store of trading goods, [tendered] them to sell; of whom they [the Plymouth traders] bought a good quantity. . . ."[13]

A Plymouth trader, Jonathan Brewster, appears in the records of New Amsterdam for July 29, 1647, when he made bond there for the value of 103 ells of duffel cloth delivered to him by Willem Turck, a merchant of New Amsterdam.[14]

Possibly the two New Englanders most deeply involved in trading with the Dutch were Isaac Allerton and Thomas Willett, both of whom were originally of Plymouth and connected with the New Plymouth Company. Willett, an Englishman who, like Isaac Allerton, had lived in Leyden for many years before coming to Plymouth in 1629, moved about a great deal. He was a magistrate of Plymouth from 1651 to 1664, was appointed first mayor of New York in 1665, and toward the end of his life, retired to Rhode Island, where he died. It appears that Pieter Stuyvesant trusted Willett completely and appointed him as one of the commissioners to decide on the boundary between New Netherland and New England.[15]

Isaac Allerton, a remarkable man in many respects and a controversial figure in New England, was an outstanding entrepreneur whose business extended into several of the early colonies, including Virginia. He had close ties with the Dutch, perhaps because, like theirs, his "faith in trading was unquenchable."[16] He owned property on Manhattan and resided there at intervals. His name often appears in the public records of the Dutch at Manhattan as a party to business agreements such as that of January 26, 1645, in which Han Evertsen Bout and Jan Jansz Damen gave him their power of attorney to sell the ship *St. Pieter* in New England.[17]

Although Allerton was residing in New Haven at the time of his death (February 1659), his will is almost entirely concerned with sums owed to him in guilders by citizens of New Netherland, and it is eloquent testimony of his long and intricate trading relationship with the Dutch. It mentions Thomas Willett and Augustine Heermans as arbiters in one case, and a sum in guilders, large for that time, is left in trust with Captain Willett.[18] The register kept by Salomon Lachaire, a notary of Manhattan, contains many items showing business contacts between the Dutch of New Netherland and the traders of New England towns. There appears for the year 1661 a substantial inventory of documents then in the hands of Abram van Nes, Allerton's attorney in Manhattan, relating to the aforementioned business matters.[19]

Plymouth, which had started out so bravely in its brisk Indian trade, was an early victim of the exhaustion of the beaver supply in New England. With its growth insufficient to allow it to compete with Boston in general commerce and the French and Dutch blocking the Indian trade with the west, the town of the Pilgrim Fathers became a backwater.

1. Edmund B. O'Callaghan, *History of New Netherland* (New York: D. Appleton and Co., 1848), 1:105.
2. William Bradford, *Bradford's History of Plymouth Plantation, 1606-1646*, ed. William T. Davis (New York: Charles Scribner's Sons, 1908), 224-25.
3. Ibid., 226-27.
4. Ibid., 234.
5. Ibid., 235.
6. Ibid.
7. O'Callaghan, *History of New Netherland*, 1:109-10.
8. William B. Weeden, *Economic and Social History of New England, 1620-1789* (New York: Hillary House Publishers, 1963), 1:124; Bradford, *History of Plymouth Plantation*, 234.
9. Bradford, *History of Plymouth Plantation*, 311.
10. Ibid.
11. William C. Sturtevant, ed., *Handbook of North American Indians*, vol. 15, ed. Bruce Trigger (Washington, D.C.: Smithsonian Institution, 1978), 89.
12. Bradford, *History of Plymouth Plantation*, 311.
13. Ibid., 328.
14. *New York Historical Manuscripts: Dutch*, vol. 2, *Register of the Provincial Secretary of New Netherland, 1642-1647*, ed. Kenneth Scott and Kenn Stryker-Rodda, and trans. Arnold J. F. van Laer (Baltimore: Genealogical Publishing Co., 1974), 447.
15. O'Callaghan, *Documents Relative to the Colonial History of the State of New York* (Albany: Weed, Parsons and Co., 1853-1858), 1:496.
16. *Dictionary of American Biography*, s.v. "Allerton, Isaac."
17. *New York Historical Manuscripts: Dutch*, 2:289.
18. *Mayflower Descendant* 2 (July 1900): 155-57.
19. *New York Historical Manuscripts: Dutch. The Register of Salomon Lachaire, Notary Public at New Amsterdam, 1661-1662*, ed. Kenneth Scott and Kenn Stryker-Rodda, and trans. E. B. O'Callaghan (Baltimore: Genealogical Publishing Co., 1978), 26-27.

6
Dutch Trade with Boston and the
Massachusetts Bay Settlements

Compared with the Virginia, New Netherland, and Plymouth settlements, Boston made a late entry on the American scene. Yet within the space of only a few years after its founding in 1630, that town developed into the only trading center in America that could then rival New Amsterdam. The reason for this is not far to seek. Boston, unlike either Plymouth or Virginia, was from the beginning heavily populated by the sons and relatives of members of London's mercantile class. "Blood relationships between English suppliers and New England merchants were an exceptionally useful bond,"[1] a circumstance that becomes immediately apparent in the *Aspinwall Papers*, where there are repeated references that show how this consanguinity between Boston merchants and merchants in London or Bristol greased the wheels of Boston's commerce.[2]

Boston was a middle-class town, and the motivation of the middle class from its beginnings has invariably been trade. Here, then, was a people the Dutch of New Netherland could understand and with whom they could identify. It is not surprising, therefore, that a strong trading relationship that cut through national rivalries developed quickly between these two otherwise dissimilar communities. The numerous references to this trade in the extant records of that time, both Dutch and English, give but a hint of how extensive it actually was.

The first settlers of Boston landed at Charlestown on June 12, 1630, and it is probable that they established a trade with the Dutch within a fairly short time since the nearby Plymouth colony had already set up a brisk trade with New Netherland. John Winthrop, in his journal, first mentions such contacts in May 1633, when he recorded that "a Dutch pink arrived, which had been to the southward trading."[3] In October of the same year, he noted that the bark *Blessing*, of Massachusetts Bay, had visited New Amsterdam, "where they were kindly entertained" and traded for beaver.[4]

By 1634, this trade with the Dutch was firmly established, for Winthrop notes on August 12 that "our neighbors of Plymouth and we oft trade with the Dutch at Hudson's River.... We had from them about forty sheep, and beaver, and brass pieces, and sugar, etc.... for sack, strong waters, linen cloth and other commodities."[5] Weeden says, "The [Boston] trade with the Dutch had assumed such proportions [by 1643] that a special act was passed to regulate ... their coin."[6] This concern with Dutch coinage almost certainly reflects a dearth of English money in the colony.

From the satisfaction with which Winthrop in May 1639 discusses the possibility of arriving at a better relationship with the Dutch, now that Willem Kieft had succeeded Wouter van Twiller as governor of New Netherland, it may be inferred that trade relations between Boston and Manhattan had been deteriorating. Winthrop had learned from the governor of Connecticut that the new Dutch governor appeared to be "a more discreet and sober man than the former . . . and was very forward to hold correspondency with us . . . which occasioned us the more readily to renew the former treaty, that the Dutch might not take notice of any breach or alienation between us."[7]

Throughout Winthrop's journal it is made obvious that the Massachusetts authorities sought, whenever possible, to propitiate the Dutch in order to insure good trade relationships with them. On one occasion, in June 1640, when certain inhabitants of Lynn removed themselves to an area on Long Island claimed by both Lord Stirling (William Alexander) and the Dutch, on complaint of the latter, Thomas Dudley, governor of Massachusetts, hastily disclaimed responsibility for the acts of the people from Lynn.[8]

Because of their close personal ties with the British merchants, Boston and its surrounding towns were in a better position than the other colonial settlements in America to acquire such modest consumer goods as were available from England. Certainly, the Aspinwall notarial records support the conclusion that even during the civil war years of the 1640s, supplies of small manufactures, particularly textiles and accessories for the making of clothing, were being imported into Boston on a fairly regular basis. The war, along with Boston's lack of credit in London, however, seriously restricted this trade, and it appears that the goods that came in were neither sufficient in quantity nor suited enough to the Indian taste to supply adequately the demands of the fur trade. Nor were they plentiful enough to furnish the overseas trade with the Caribbean, Africa, and the Wine Islands that Boston entrepreneurs were determined to embark upon, and which the distraction of England by its civil war left them free to pursue.[9]

In addition, Boston needed ships, and while it would eventually build them, for the time it saw in the Dutch a source that could be immediately tapped for bottoms. It is not surprising, then, that Dutch records for this period contain abundant references to the sale or charter of ships to New Englanders. One such is a record of September 1640. When the Dutch galliot de Bruyt (out of Enckhuysen, Isaack Abrahamsen, master) was seized at New Amsterdam under suspicion of smuggling, Governor Winthrop informed the authorities there that the ship had already been sold to Robert Scott and John Cook, merchants of Boston.[10]

In another transaction in 1647, Pieter Stuyvesant and Willem Kieft, officials of the West India Company in Manhattan, sold the company ship Amandare to Thomas Broughton of Watertown, Massachusetts. Isaac Allerton, then apparently living at least some of the time in New Amsterdam, and Thomas Willett of Plymouth were sureties and coprincipals.[11] The sum involved, 10,000 guilders, was a large one for that time.[12] Three years later, "Thomas Broughton of Watertown, merchant," gave a power of attorney to Captain Thomas Willett to collect from "Mijn Heere Peter Stuyvesant" money owed on the account of the Amandare.[13] The mere logistics of this trading in ships between the Dutch and the New Englanders constituted an additional impetus for their economic cooperation.

Ships were often chartered from the Dutch by the merchants of the Massachusetts Bay community. In March 1649, William Aspinwall, notary, attested that at the request of Ralph Whory of Charlestown, he filed a protest with Peter Clawson [Pieter Claessen],[14] master of the ship Ganatree of Hoorn (Holland), and Jacob Petersen, merchant and owner of that ship, for "breach of charter party."[15] In October of the same year, James Neale, merchant of Boston, contracted with Christopher Johnson [Christoffel Jansen], master of the ship Orangetree of Amsterdam, to charter Jansen's craft for freighting a cargo from Virginia to Lisbon.[16]

In April 1650, papers concerning differences between John Peters [Jan Pietersz], master of the ship Fortuyn, and John Parris of Massachusetts Bay were presented for arbitration. This matter involved a cargo of iron that Parris had bought from Pietersz, and the decision was that Parris must pay £14 a ton, unless "the said John Peters can make it appear it cost more in Holland." At the time of this arbitration, the Fortuyn was "rideing at Anchor in the Charles River." The principals in this contract were also involved in a charter of the Fortuyn for a voyage to Guinea and Barbados in connection with the slave trade.[17] The same John Parris had earlier shipped goods with Maerten Jacobsz, master of the ship St. Maerten, bound for Madeira. To this particular contract, Maerten Jacobsz appended a signed statement in Dutch.[18] Jacobsz appears as a principal in other contracts made at Boston.

Existing records of New Netherland likewise indicate a long trading association between the Dutch there and merchants of the Boston area. An entry of 1638 shows that Willem Kieft, director of New Netherland, gave Samuel Maverick of Boston a power of attorney to collect from Boston merchants monies previously due the West India Company.[19] The records also show that at this time Isaac Allerton owned a trading bark that made frequent trips between Boston and New Amsterdam.

One New Netherland legal document of 1647 attesting to the large scale of many of these commercial enterprises between the Dutch and the people of Massachusetts Bay concerns freight charges on two ships, one belonging to the Dutch West India Company and the other to Willem de Key, a merchant of New Amsterdam. Ralph Whory of Charlestown was a principal in this affair; John Browne of Salem, Thomas Willett of Plymouth, and Isaac Allerton appeared as witnesses.[20] In another record, the Council of New Netherland voted in June 1647 to send the ship Groote Gerrit, Jelmer Tomassen, master, to Boston laden with lumber to be sold "for the highest price possible" and there to take on a cargo of provisions to be sold later in Curaçao.[21]

Complaining against Director Stuyvesant in 1649, a group of citizens of New Amsterdam charged that "worthy and reliable people who come thence here by way of Boston, and others trading hence to Boston, assure us that more than 25 ships would come annually here from the Islands were they not afraid of confiscation," and they declared Stuyvesant to be "sorely destructive of the prosperity of New Netherland."[22] The islands here referred to may have been the Spanish and Portuguese Wine Islands, with which Boston carried on a brisk trade, much of it in Dutch ships. A further complaint made against the director of New Netherland the following year declared that he had appointed Englishmen to high civil and military offices and "hath sold the [West India] Company's guns and cannon, with all sorts of munitions of war, to the English at Boston."[23]

The First Anglo-Dutch War (1652-1653) affected commerce as adversely for Boston as for all the English colonies. Both sides were quick to fit out privateers to prey on each other. David Selleck, a prominent merchant of Boston, applied for letters of marque for four of these ships. At about the same time, John Hull, another Boston merchant, complained that he had had two ships taken by the Dutch, with great loss in goods. However, no lasting rancor appears to have been generated by these or subsequent Anglo-Dutch hostilities, and as soon as they were officially over, the Dutch and English resumed trading with one another, cheerfully ignoring such trade laws as Parliament or the States General saw fit to put in their way.

Thus, it appears that the Dutch trade with Boston did not conclude with the end of Dutch colonial power in America any more than it had with the other English settlements. In England in 1676 the Lords of Trade became especially concerned with what they saw as New England's intransigence in the matter of subscribing to English trade regulations. They sent over Edward Randolph to look into the matter, and he arrived in Boston in May of that year. In his report, Randolph charged that

> there is no notice taken of the act of navigation, plantation, or any other lawes made in England for the regulation of trade. All nations having free liberty to come into their ports and vend their commodities, without any restraint; and in this as well as in other things, that government [Massachusetts] would make the world believe they are a free state and doe act in all matters accordingly, and doe presume to give passports to ships, not only belonging to that colony but also to England, without any regard to those rules prescribed by his Majestie.[24]

That the Dutch figured prominently among the "nations having free liberty" to come into the Massachusetts ports cannot be doubted by anyone who understands the trading proclivities of the Dutch or the long tradition of their trading relationship with Boston.

The diary that Kiliaen van Rensselaer, third patroon of the *colonie* of Rensselaerswyck, kept on his voyage to New York from Amsterdam in 1685 shows that the Dutch ship carrying him docked first at Boston and remained there for four days before proceeding to Manhattan.[25] This is but one among the many pieces of evidence that Dutch trade with Boston continued long beyond the New Netherland years.

Notes - Chapter 6

1. Bernard Bailyn, *The New England Merchants in the Seventeenth Century* (New York: Harper and Row, 1964), 35.
2. William Aspinwall, *A Volume Relating to the Early History of Boston Containing the Aspinwall Notarial Records from 1644 to 1651* [*Aspinwall Papers*] (Boston: Municipal Printing Office, 1903). These published papers are records kept by the notary William Aspinwall of Boston between 1644 and 1651. Aspinwall, who was returning to England, referred to them as "my notarial booke," and declared that they were "no publick Records . . . but privat Records of my own Acts." He agreed, however, to turn them over to his friend Edward Winslow, who was to rule on what should be done with such papers in the event of a notary's leaving the province.
3. John Winthrop, *Journal, 1630-1649*, ed. James K. Hosmer (New York: Charles Scribner's Sons, 1908), 1:102.
4. Ibid., 109.
5. Ibid.
6. William B. Weeden, *Economic and Social History of New England, 1620-1789* (New York: Hillary House Publishers, 1963), 1:143.
7. Winthrop, *Journal*, 1:301-2.
8. Ibid., 2:4-5.
9. Bailyn, *New England Merchants*, 93.
10. *New York Historical Manuscripts: Dutch*, vol. 5, *Council Minutes, 1652-1654*, ed. and trans. Charles T. Gehring (Baltimore: Genealogical Publishing Co., 1983), 8-9.
11. New Netherland records show that Isaac Allerton was prominent in New Amsterdam as early as 1638 and that he owned property there jointly with Govert Loockermans, a Dutchman deeply involved in trade with Boston and other parts of New England. Thomas Willett also owned real property in New Amsterdam. (*New York Historical Manuscripts: Dutch*, vols. GG, HH & II, *Land Papers* [*1632-1664*], ed. and trans. Charles T. Gehring [Baltimore: Genealogical Publishing Co., 1980], 31.)
12. *New York Historical Manuscripts: Dutch*, vol. 2, *Register of the Provincial Secretary of New Netherland, 1642-1647*, ed. Kenneth Scott and Kenn Stryker-Rodda, and trans. Arnold J. F. van Laer (Baltimore: Genealogical Publishing Co., 1974), 401.

13. [*Aspinwall Papers*], 277.
14. In their original records, both the Dutch and the English gave their own spelling to proper names. Because of this, the correct nationalities sometimes go undiscovered.
15. [*Aspinwall Papers*], 218-19.
16. Ibid., 243.
17. Ibid., 290-92.
18. Ibid., 292.
19. *New York Historical Manuscripts: Dutch*, vol. 1, *Register of the Provincial Secretary of New Netherland, 1638-1642*, ed. Kenneth Scott and Kenn Stryker-Rodda, and trans. Arnold J. F. van Laer (Baltimore: Genealogical Publishing Co., 1974), 53.
20. *New York Historical Manuscripts: Dutch*, vol. 3, *Register of the Provincial Secretary of New Netherland, 1648-1660*, ed. Kenneth Scott and Kenn Stryker-Rodda, and trans. Arnold J. F. van Laer (Baltimore: Genealogical Publishing Co., 1974), 428.
21. *New York Historical Manuscripts: Dutch*, vol. 4, *Council Minutes, 1638-1649*, ed. Kenneth Scott and Kenn Stryker-Rodda, and trans. Arnold J. F. van Laer (Baltimore: Genealogical Publishing Co., 1974), 379.
22. Edmund B. O'Callaghan, *Documents Relative to the Colonial History of the State of New York* (Albany: Weed, Parsons and Co., 1853-1858), 1:313.
23. Ibid., 442.
24. Bailyn, *New England Merchants*, 157.
25. Albany Institute of History and Art, Albany, N.Y., Manuscript FG807.

7
Dutch Trade with Rhode Island

Dutch trading contacts with the area to which they gave the name *Roode Eylant* (Red Island)[1] appear to have begun prior to its settlement in 1636 by Europeans, as part of the ubiquitous Dutch trading operations along the northeastern coastline of North America. A document in the Royal Dutch Archives at the Hague, addressed to the States General by the deputies from New Netherland in July 1649, minces no words in claiming Dutch priorities in the exploration of this area and in the assigning of Dutch place names. It points out that

> all the islands, bay, harbors, rivers, kills and places . . . have Dutch names, which were given them, long before they had any others, by our Dutch navigators and traders when they first began to discover and trade to those parts. The English themselves are well aware of this, but as long as they can manage it . . . they will not admit the fact. . . .[2]

Two of the earliest focal points of Dutch trading interest in the Rhode Island area seem to have been Fort Ninigret, at what is now Charlestown, Rhode Island, and the nearby island of Quetenis. Writing some years ago about the origins of Fort Ninigret, William B. Goodwin had this to say:

> In searching the historical archives of the settlement and occupation by the Dutch West India Company, from 1623 to 1674, of that part of New England and New York, originally known as the Dutch New Netherlands, the writer came across two salient excerpts which led him to believe that there must have been a somewhat earlier Dutch trading station and/or fort in the Narragansett Country in Rhode Island than has hitherto been generally accepted.[3]

Goodwin proceeds to quote from several sources pointing to Dutch ownership of a fort here prior to the Dutch purchase, in 1636-37, of the island called by the Indians "Quetenis." The first of these references is a letter written in 1631 by the Dutch ambassador to England, in which he declares that before 1630 the Dutch had a fort and colony in the Narragansett area "which has been continuously occupied."[4]

This and other documentary sources that he believed pointed to early Dutch settlement at Narra-

gansett Bay prompted Goodwin to apply to the Metropolitan Park Commission for permission to make a test archaeological exploration in the Charlestown area. This produced artifacts that were later identified as Dutch, and Mr. Goodwin concluded "that there is a strong possibility" that the Dutch built Fort Ninigret after 1627 and before 1637 but abandoned it when their trade was disrupted by the war that broke out between the Narragansett and Pequot Indians, around 1635.[5]

Other researchers have disagreed with the opinion that Ninigret was at one time a Dutch fort. Bert Salwen and Susan Mayer, who made a test excavation there in the late 1970s, believe that it was built by the Niantic Indians, who were "obviously in frequent contact with Europeans," and that Ninigret was "primarily a trading center."[6] Several of the artifacts they recovered there appear to be of Dutch origin, and Paul R. Huey[7] has identified one of these—a heavily ornamented circlet of brass—as being identical to an artifact recovered from the Dutch ship *Batavia*, which sank in western Australian waters in 1629,[8] a date consistent with Goodwin's conclusions about the probable period in which the Dutch built Fort Ninigret.

Corroboration of the Dutch purchase of the island Quetenis can be found in several documents preserved at the Hague. In a description of the boundaries of New Netherland written in February 1651, Pieter Stuyvesant claimed for it "the island named Quetenis, lying in Sloop Bay, which was purchased, paid for and taken possession of in the year 1637 on the [West India] Company's account."[9] A further memoir of the West India Company of December 30, 1654, declared that the Dutchman Abraham Pietersen of Haarlem had occupied Quetenis in 1636 and had taken possession of the surrounding territory in that year.[10] In a protest against the English takeover of New Netherland in 1664, the Dutch reaffirm this, pointing out that Quetenis is "still and at this day called by the English themselves The Dutchman's Island."[11]

It appears that the trade between the Dutch and the Rhode Island settlers was marked by less tension than that of the Dutch with Connecticut although, as we have seen, the Dutch early laid claim to the territory that is Rhode Island and continued to reiterate this claim. A West India Company review, dated November 5, 1660, of the long-standing problem of English encroachments on Dutch-claimed territory in New England states that the Dutch had taken possession of Rhode Island and surrounding areas in 1636.[12]

Such protests were, however, more in the nature of diplomatic exchanges between the States General and the Court of St. James than actual confrontations between the nationals of these countries in America. When the director at New Amsterdam was vocal in these claims, it was by virtue of his official position as the representative in America of the Dutch West India Company. For their part, the Rhode Islanders, because of their liberal religious and political views, may have been more congenial with the Dutch than with the people of Massachusetts Bay.

Roger Williams founded Providence in 1636 and quickly established a good relationship with the Narragansett Indians. The new colony turned to trade with the Indians as the most immediately available source of income, but traders must have goods to distribute, and these were in short supply. If the well-established merchants of Boston, in spite of their close personal ties with the mercantile fraternity of London, were finding it difficult to obtain supplies, what sources could such outlanders as Williams and his followers hope to tap?

It appears that the answer was the Dutch, and several factors made this feasible. One was the geographical proximity of Rhode Island to Manhattan; another was that the Dutch in their pragmatism were not in the habit of allowing religious or political differences to interfere with trade; and, finally, there was the inclination of the Dutch to trade wherever and whenever an opportunity presented itself.

In 1642 England was in political turmoil. In January of that year the king sent an armed force onto the floor of the House of Commons with orders to arrest Pym, Hampden, and other leaders of the opposition. The English Commons was traditionally off-limits to the king or his agents, and although the men sought were not arrested because they were not there, the unprecedented royal move was the overture to civil war, which broke out a few months later.

In any such struggle the liberal Rhode Islanders would naturally sympathize with the Commonwealth party, but their first need was to secure their own economic survival. Thus, as if on cue, the General Court for Newport, on September 18, 1642,

ordered the governor to "treat with the Dutch to supply us with necessaries, and to take of our commodities at such rates as may be suitable."[13]

Thus, throughout the 1640s, because of the tensions in England leading up to the civil war and then the war itself, Rhode Island, like the other New England colonies, had not only more freedom from supervision than it would have had in a more normal era, but also more need to establish markets elsewhere because of England's neglect stemming from its preoccupation with its internal struggle. When from necessity the Rhode Islanders turned to the Dutch, certain prominent Rhode Island merchants and captains took the lead in establishing close trading connections with New Netherland. Carl Bridenbaugh names among these William Coddington, William Brenton, John Underhill, and John Throgmorton, while on the Dutch side he notes Skippers Arent Isaacsz and Cornelis Melyn.[14] These names Bridenbaugh took from official Rhode Island records of the period. He declares that "throughout the forties, most of the growing carrying trade between New Netherland and Rhode Island went on in Dutch bottoms."[15]

Other names of prominent traders may be culled from extant records of New Netherland. The court and notarial records of the Dutch in New Amsterdam make repeated reference to Captain Jeremy Clarke (he signed his name "Clerk"), a prominent merchant of Newport, and Captain Richard Smith, who, though a resident of Rhode Island, also maintained a house on Manhattan. Smith had first settled in the Plymouth colony, but because of religious differences with his neighbors there, he had subsequently moved to Rhode Island.[16] In these records, the name of the former is usually written "Clercq," while that of the latter appears with the Dutch spelling "Smit." In the register of the secretary of New Netherland there is an agreement between "Captain Jeremias Clerck" and "Jan Domer" (John Dummer, of Boston) signed in New Amsterdam on June 19, 1647, that concerns a note which Dummer had given to Clarke but which subsequently came into the hands of Captain Richard Smith, who had sued Dummer in the New Amsterdam courts. Dummer appears to have commanded a bark and crew that traded along the Atlantic seaboard.[17]

In addition to Jeremy Clarke and Richard Smith, whose names appear again and again in the Manhattan records as traders, there was another group of merchants, originally from Boston but sympathetic to the dissenters, who had followed Mrs. Anne Hutchinson to Rhode Island and who almost certainly traded with the Dutch.[18] Another Dutchman, Jochem Kierstede of New Amsterdam, was trading with Rhode Island prior to October 1, 1645, as we learn from a suit against him filed by Juriaen Blanck and our old friend Thomas Willett, also residents of Manhattan.[19]

An item involving mistaken identity in the council minutes of New Netherland for May 2, 1648, shows the casualness with which the Dutch pursued their periodically illegal trade with southern New England. Govert Aertsen, who had gone with his sloop to trade in Rhode Island and Connecticut, was threatened with arrest by the Rhode Island authorities. They had apparently mistaken him for Govert Loockermans, another New Netherland citizen who was accused of selling contraband powder and lead to the Indians of Rhode Island. Aertsen asked the council for a certificate of identity so that he could carry on his Rhode Island trade in safety.[20]

Although the First Anglo-Dutch War began in May 1652, Rhode Island appears to have continued its usual trade with the Dutch throughout that year and into 1653, when the trade was prohibited.[21] This prohibition seems to have been unpopular, at least in Providence, where the citizens objected to it heatedly, claiming that they "knew not for what reasons" the decree had been issued.[22]

A few Rhode Islanders, however, obviously saw in the war a chance to get rich. These applied for and received commissions from the English government to engage in privateering operations against Dutch shipping. This also disturbed the people of Providence, who, on June 27, 1654, dispatched a letter to Sir Henry Vane complaining about one of these privateers, William Dyre, who seems to have gotten somewhat carried away. They declared that Dyre "plungeth himself and some others, in most unnecessary and unrighteous plunderings, both of Dutch and French and English; all to our grief, who protested against such abuse [privateering permission] from England. . . ."[23]

The war ended in April 1653. It is not recorded when the law against trading with the Dutch was repealed in Providence, but Newport did not repeal it until May 1657, nor did Warwick until May 1658.[24] Perhaps the Dutch trade had become a local political issue, which may explain why some towns were tardy in legalizing it, but this is unsupported speculation. On the other hand, it is by no means certain that the Dutch trade with Rhode Island ever entirely stopped during the war years even though it was undoubtedly reduced. Presumably, too, the Navigation Act of 1651 was still in force, but how much it contributed to restricting the Dutch trade in Rhode Island is problematical. Bridenbaugh says:

> And despite the ban on all Dutch traffic with the Indians of Rhode Island during the first Dutch War . . . , John Garious (Garriad, Gariardy, Gerard), possibly a Fleming, who married the sister of John Warner of Warwick, traded for furs with Ezekiel Holliman and John Greene, Jr., on the west shore of the bay. A few Rhode Islanders, notably John Throgmorton (whose name is perpetuated at Throgs Neck in Westchester County), made voyages to Manhattan in their shallops with some regularity.[25]

The coming of members of the Society of Friends to Rhode Island in 1657 was another factor that contributed to the Dutch trade with that colony, since the Quakers had every reason to dislike and distrust the powerful Massachusetts Bay merchants. In May 1657, the General Assembly of Rhode Island resolved that "the Dutch may have lawfull commerce with the English in this Collony, correspondent to the peace in beinge between the nations."[26] The following year, in May, the same General Assembly forbade the seizure of Dutch ships in Narragansett Bay, except by a special order from England or by an order of the General Assembly itself.[27]

There is every reason to believe that in the 1660s trade between the Dutch and the merchants of Rhode Island proceeded with as much regularity as it had in the previous decade. In 1664 the English seized New Netherland from the Dutch at a time when the two countries were not officially at war, and this sparked the Second Anglo-Dutch War, which was declared in June 1665. The Rhode Islanders continued to trade with Manhattan as if no changes had taken place on the political scene since none had taken place on the mercantile one. The Dutch merchants of Manhattan were still ordering and receiving from Holland and the Wine Islands the consumer goods that the Rhode Islanders, who had a surprisingly high standard of living, preferred, and the latter were still buying these from the Dutch.[28] There is no reason to doubt that this trade continued with only minor interruptions through the Third Anglo-Dutch War, which ended in February 1674.

It would seem, therefore, in view of the foregoing documentary evidence, that of all the New England colonies, no other had a more sustained and cordial trade relationship with the Dutch than Rhode Island.

1. This, the largest island in Narragansett Bay, was originally called Aquidneck and is now Newport County, according to the Official Gazetteer of Rhode Island, 1932. In Dutch the double "o" is pronounced as in "rode."

2. Edmund B. O'Callaghan, *Documents Relative to the Colonial History of the State of New York* (Albany: Weed, Parsons and Co., 1853-1858), 1:285.

3. William B. Goodwin, "Notes Regarding the Origin of Fort Ninigret in the Narragansett Country at Charlestown," *Rhode Island Historical Society Collections* 25 (January 1932): 1. Goodwin gives no citation by which his reference may be verified, and the author has not been able to do so, yet there seems no reason to question the existence of such an English/Dutch diplomatic paper.

4. Goodwin, "Origin of Fort Ninigret," 2.

5. Ibid., 15; Swanton declares that "around" 1635 the Narragansetts, warring with the Pequots, drove them from a small area in Rhode Island that they were occupying. (John R. Swanton, *The Indian Tribes of North America*, Bureau of American Ethnology Bulletin, no. 145 [Washington, D.C.: Smithsonian Institution, 1952], 32.)

6. Bert Salwen and Susan N. Mayer, "Indian Archaeology in Rhode Island," *Archaeology* 31 (1978): 57-58.

7. Mr. Huey, an archaeologist with the New York State Office of Parks, Recreation and Historic Preservation, directed the excavation of Fort Orange (Albany, New York) in 1970-71. He is an authority on seventeenth-century Dutch artifacts.

8. Myra Stanbury, comp., *Batavia Catalog* (Perth, Australia: Western Australian Museum, 1974), BAT. 3132.

9. O'Callaghan, *Colonial History of the State of New York,* 1:544.

10. Ibid., 565.

11. Ibid., 2:409.

12. Ibid., 2:134.

13. John R. Bartlett, ed., *Records of the Colony of Rhode Island and Providence Plantations, in New England, 1636-1663* (Providence: A. Crawford Greene and Brother, 1856-1865), 1:126.

14. Carl Bridenbaugh, *Fat Mutton and Liberty of Conscience* (Providence: Brown University Press, 1974), 23.

15. Ibid.

16. J. Franklin Jameson, ed., *Narratives of New Netherland, 1609-1664* (New York: Charles Scribner's Sons, 1909), 266 fn.

17. *New York Historical Manuscripts: Dutch,* vol. 2, *Register of the Provincial Secretary of New Netherland, 1642-1647,* ed. Kenneth Scott and Kenn Stryker-Rodda, and trans. Arnold J. F. van Laer (Baltimore: Genealogical Publishing Co., 1974), 413-14.

18. Bernard Bailyn, *The New England Merchants in the Seventeenth Century* (New York: Harper and Row, 1964), 40-41.

19. *New York Historical Manuscripts: Dutch,* vol. 4, *Council Minutes, 1638-1649,* ed. Kenneth Scott and Kenn Stryker-Rodda, and trans. Arnold J. F. van Laer (Baltimore: Genealogical Publishing Co., 1974), 285.

20. Ibid., 519.

21. Bartlett, *Records of the Colony of Rhode Island,* 1:261.

22. Ibid., 270-71.

23. Ibid., 288.

24. Ibid., 356, 389.

25. Bridenbaugh, *Fat Mutton and Liberty of Conscience,* 23.

26. Ibid., 61.

27. Ibid.

28. Ibid., 112.

8
Dutch Trade with Connecticut

In consequence of clashes of interest between the Dutch and the Connecticut settlers on the north shore of Long Island, on the South (Delaware) River, and on the *Versche* (Fresh, or Connecticut) River, Dutch relations with Connecticut in the seventeenth century were stormier than with the other New England settlements. So inflamed was the situation by April 3, 1642, that on that date the Council of New Netherland forbade its citizens to trade with Connecticut on account of the English takeover of Dutch-claimed territory there[1]—a most significant action when it is considered that the Dutch rarely let hostilities between themselves and others interfere with trade.

Extant seventeenth-century records of the Dutch and of the Connecticut colony contain charges and countercharges concerning conflicting claims on Long Island, Connecticut's attempt to infiltrate the fur trade on the South River, the loss of Fort Good Hope to the English, and other matters of contention between the two. These conflicts are too tedious and too far out of the realm of this study to be treated at length here, but they contributed to an atmosphere of dislike and distrust between the Dutch and Connecticut that was detrimental to a good trade relationship between them. Ultimately, both the wrangling and the trade between the two continued throughout the seventeenth century.

There is a certain amount of confusion about when the Dutch first made a settlement on the *Versche* (Connecticut) River. In a deposition made in 1688, many years after the event, Catelijn Trico states that in 1623 [error for 1624] she came with a group of colonists to New Netherland, and upon their arrival at Manhattan, the officials there sent "two families & six men to har'ford River" to settle, while others were sent to Albany.[2] Since the Dutch record of the building of Fort Good Hope in 1633 on the site of the present Hartford, Connecticut,[3] is clearly repeated in more than one seventeenth-century document, it is possible that the settlers of 1624 were withdrawn a short time later, as were those in Albany, and that no other permanent Dutch settlement was made in Connecticut until the building of Fort Good Hope in 1633.

Shortly after this, certain English colonists who had become dissatisfied with conditions in Massachusetts made settlements in the Connecticut River valley at Wethersfield (1634-35), Windsor (1635), and Hartford (1635). In the same year, a settlement sponsored by an English company headed by Lords Say and Brooke was made at the mouth of the Connecticut River and was named Saybrook to honor the founders. Another group, also at odds with authority in Massachusetts, founded New Haven in 1638. This place the Dutch called *Roodeberch* (Red Hill), and the number of references to it in New Netherland public records indicates a good commerce between the two places in spite of their differences. In the end, the Dutch West India Company was unable or unwilling to give the Dutch at Fort Good Hope sufficient military support to contain the momentum of the English movement into the Connecticut Valley. As a result, the Dutch were finally forced to give up that trading site in 1654.

Numerous small items in the public records, however, testify to persistent trading contacts throughout the New Netherland years between individual citizens of New Netherland and of Connecticut. Typical of these transactions is one in 1647 in which Richard Lord, an Englishman residing on the Fresh (Connecticut) River, sold a large quantity of pork to Adriaen de Keyser, a prominent citizen of Manhattan, with payment to be made at Boston;[4] or another of 1649, when Jan Harmensen of New Amsterdam ordered through another New Netherland trader three pipes of brandy from the magistrates of New Haven. In that year, too, a New Netherland court ordered that the debts owed the estate of Claes Cater of New Amsterdam be collected from persons in New Haven, Stamford, and Milford, Connecticut.[5] Although such items are insignificant in themselves, it is believed that they represent the tip of a larger iceberg of trade that rarely found its way into the public records, sometimes probably because it was pursued illegally.

Indications that the Dutch of New Netherland traded whenever possible with the Indians of Connecticut surface here and there in the records. A vessel owned by Augustine Heermans of the South River settlements was trading with those around Saybrook in May 1651; on May 20, 1652, a Connecticut court considered the seizure of another vessel, belonging to a Dutchman named Oulsterman, that was trading at Fairfield.[6] Govert Loockermans, the prominent New Amsterdam trader mentioned earlier in connection with illicit trade in Rhode Island, is another who received somewhat dubious notice in the records for his involvement in commerce with Connecticut Indians.[7]

As in the case of Massachusetts, contracts involving the exchange of ships between New Netherland and Connecticut appear often enough in the court records to indicate a brisk trade in that area. In a bill of sale of September 1647, Pieter Stuyvesant conveyed to Stephen Goodyear, deputy governor of New Haven, the former West India Company ship *Swol*.[8]

An interesting sequel to the sale of the *Swol* reveals another facet of the Dutch trade with Connecticut— that originating in Holland. As has been indicated earlier, a certain amount of Dutch trade with New England communities was carried on sub rosa by Dutch free traders operating out of the fatherland. In 1647, shortly after the sale of the *Swol* but before her

delivery to New Haven, Cornelis Claesen Snoy, master of the ship *St. Beninjo*, a Dutch free-trading vessel then lying at New Haven, asked permission of the New Netherland authorities to proceed to New Amsterdam to trade. Although this would be in violation of the monopoly, Stuyvesant granted the request on the grounds that he had no means of forcibly seizing the *St. Beninjo* and that the local merchants might as well profit from the trade.[9] A short time later, the master and one of the owners of the *St. Beninjo* arrived in Manhattan on Govert Aertsen's sloop, having left their ship in New Haven. The New Netherland authorities had by this time established that the ship's cargo included contraband in the form of guns and powder, and they decided on a plan to seize her. Since the *Swol* was scheduled to be delivered to its new owner in New Haven, they determined to equip that craft with a fighting crew and ammunition sufficient to take the *St. Beninjo* by force and bring her to Manhattan—an enterprise subsequently accomplished.[10]

The General Court of Connecticut, on July 11, 1654, repealed an earlier "order of restraint of trade with the Dutch & other foreigne natyons."[11] Thus, though relations between New Netherland and Connecticut were at times less cordial than those of the Dutch with the other English colonies because of rather bitter competition for territory and the Indian trade, it is obvious that the merchants of Connecticut were unwilling to have these contacts end.

Notes - Chapter 8

1. *New York Historical Manuscripts: Dutch,* vol. 4, *Council Minutes, 1638-1649,* ed. Kenneth Scott and Kenn Stryker-Rodda, and trans. Arnold J. F. van Laer (Baltimore: Geneaological Publishing Co., 1974), 140.
2. New York State Library, Albany, New York Colonial Manuscripts, 35:182. The notary who took this deposition wrote the name in the Dutch manner, *Catelijn,* and she signed with her mark. She is known, however, to history as Catelina Trico. Modern historians tend to discount her testimony because it contains anachronisms in the use of Iroquois names and because of the suspicion that her memory was being influenced by Dongan for political reasons. (See George T. Hunt, *The Wars of the Iroquois* [Madison: University of Wisconsin Press, 1940], 28-30.) It seems likely, however, that her facts about the families and men sent to the Connecticut River area are true.
3. Edmund B. O'Callaghan, *Documents Relative to the Colonial History of the State of New York* (Albany: Weed, Parsons and Co., 1853-1858), 2:140. The name of this Dutch trading post appears in contemporary seventeenth-century documents in several forms: Fort *Hoop,* Fort *Goed Hoop,* and *der Hoop.* (Information from Charles T. Gehring.)
4. *New York Historical Manuscripts: Dutch,* vol. 2, *Register of the Provincial Secretary of New Netherland, 1642-1647,* ed. Kenneth Scott and Kenn Stryker-Rodda, and trans. Arnold J. F. van Laer (Baltimore: Genealogical Publishing Co., 1974), 421.
5. (F.W.B.), "Inter-Colony Trading," *de Halve Maen* 55 (Spring 1980): 21.
6. F. Hammond Trumbull, ed., *The Public Records of the Colony of Connecticut* (Hartford: Brown and Parsons, 1850), 1:219, 231.
7. *New York Historical Manuscripts: Dutch,* 4:519.
8. *New York Historical Manuscripts: Dutch,* 2:489.
9. *New York Historical Manuscripts: Dutch,* 4:435, 453.
10. Ibid., 453-60.
11. Trumbull, *Records of the Colony of Connecticut,* 1:261.

Dutch Trade with New York after 1664

In August 1664, while England and the Netherlands were officially at peace, an English fleet sailed into the harbor at New Amsterdam and claimed the territory of New Netherland for James, Duke of York and Albany, brother of Charles II. Since the Dutch authorities in New Netherland had no military reserves, Pieter Stuyvesant, Dutch director general, finally had no choice but to surrender.

British sovereignty over the province was thus established, but political, financial, and social power remained in the hands of the wealthy Dutch trading families of New York City and Albany, who had long-existing and close commercial ties with Holland and who had no intention of giving up their European markets. Equally important to them was Amsterdam's credit and banking system, the most advanced in Europe and vastly superior to that employed by the British mercantile world. In addition, there was the opulent assortment of goods available to them in Amsterdam's great warehouses, drawn from such far-flung places as the Baltic countries and the Spice Islands of Southeast Asia. Finally, among the advantages they did not wish to give up was the convenience of carrying on overseas business in their mother tongue.

It was not only the merchants of New York and Albany, however, who wanted the trade with Amsterdam to continue. Though the Indians had in the early years been naive about European values and had thus often been cheated by the traders, they had now become more discriminating concerning Dutch goods and had developed strong preferences with regard to these. As early as 1628, in a communication to West India Company officials dispatched from New Netherland, Isaack de Rasière spoke of the need for duffels, a popular cloth with which he hoped to lure the French Indians to Fort Orange to trade, and then said further:

> I have only about 30 pieces of cloth that are in colors that are in demand, that is blue and standard gray; the rest which I have are all red, whereof I can hardly sell a yard, because the Indians say that it hinders them in hunting, being visible too far off. They all call for black, the darker the color the better, but red and green they will not take....

> ...the Indians will be all the more diligent in hunting when they see that when they have skins they can get what they want... about which the Maquaes [Mohawks] do not hesitate to complain bitterly....[1]

That this matter of Indian preference in trade goods was still a vital consideration nearly forty years later for the Dutch merchants of New York is clear from a passage in a proposal that Pieter Stuyvesant sent to James, Duke of York, in 1667:

> Since the Trade of Beaver, (the most desirable comodity for Europe) hath allwayes been purchased from the Indyans, by the Comodities brought from Holland as Camper, Duffles, Hatchetts, and other Iron worke made at Utrick &c much esteemed of by the Natives, It is to be fear'd that if those Comodities should fail them, the very Trade itself would fall....[2]

Equally, the tastes of the women of New York, almost entirely of Dutch or other continental European stock, had an appreciable influence on the pressure to continue the importation of goods from Holland. Following the English conquest of the province, there had been no rush of English people to settle there, so the English population was limited to the soldiers of the several small garrisons and a handful of British officials. Except for the few wives that accompanied the latter to America, English women were absent, and the Englishmen, from highest to lowest, took wives from among the Dutch population. These women had from infancy been accustomed to Dutch-made or Dutch-distributed goods and would certainly have initially resisted the introduction of unfamiliar household articles.

But it was not only the Dutch and Indian elements in New York that dedicated themselves to maintaining the status quo of the Dutch trade in the years beyond 1664. Faced with pressures of many kinds and receiving only a modicum of support from their own government, successive English governors saw in cooperation with the more influential elements of New York society a way to reduce the stresses of their own positions, and entered into a kind of benevolent collusion with the merchants to continue the Dutch trade.

Richard Nicolls, the first English governor of New York, in the beginning of his administration warned the British government of the need for the regular dispatch of merchant ships with consumer goods to New York if it did not wish Amsterdam to continue to dominate the commerce of the province. When Britain ignored this advice and failed to provide adequate shipments, Nicolls shifted his support to the Dutch merchants and even helped them, by proposing a plan for circumventing the British Navigation Acts.[3] According to Kupp, "Apparently the English government was reluctant to reopen a gap for evasion of the Trade and Navigation Acts after successfully closing it by the conquest of the Dutch colony . . . [but] in reality trade went on as usual despite the newly erected barriers . . . [and] with the exception of the year 1665, supplies were regularly dispatched from Holland and arrived in the Harbor of New York in Dutch ships sometimes numbering four to eight in one year."[4]

The next two governors, Francis Lovelace (1668-1673) and Edmund Andros (1674-1681), followed the lead of Nicolls in supporting the Dutch trade. This seemingly uncharacteristic behavior of the three governors stemmed from a situation that was largely the fault of their own government—failure to support adequately, either in funds or in goods, the provincial authorities. It was history repeating itself, since the Dutch West India Company had failed to support New Netherland in much the same way. As Ritchie points out, the governors were left to depend largely on local taxation for financial support of the province and on Dutch goods for carrying on the all-important Indian trade. They could not afford to antagonize the powerful local merchants when they so needed their political and commercial support.

In 1667 Pieter Stuyvesant, now in Holland, dispatched the previously quoted proposal to the Duke of York, at that time proprietor of the province of New York. In this he declared that the original Articles of Agreement between Nicolls and himself, made at the time New Netherland was surrendered to the British, provided that "the Dutch nation [in New York] should have liberty to Trade with their owne Correspondents in Holland, and have free leave to send thither what goods they please, and have returnes from thence in shipps of their owne Country."[5]

In the same document, Stuyvesant pointed out that since it appeared that no ships were scheduled to carry supplies from England to New York to tide inhabitants over the coming winter, it was necessary that ships from Holland be allowed to perform this necessary function. He asked that two ships from Holland, the *Crosse Heart* and the *Indian*, be allowed to sail immediately, declaring that if the inhabitants of the former New Netherland were not supplied with trade goods and domestic commodities, they could not continue to subsist, but must of necessity "forsake their Tillage and seeke out a Livelyhood elsewhere."[6]

By taking New York and Albany, the English had at one stroke acquired two of the three most important fur-trading centers in America (the other being Montreal). Yet in order to exploit the economic resources of their new territory, they needed the fur-trading expertise of the Dutch population. Implicit in Stuyvesant's message was the threat to the British government that should the Dutch of New York be forced to emigrate, it was not only the "tillage" that would be abandoned, but the fur trade as well.

About the same time that Stuyvesant was pointing out these home truths to the duke, he addressed a petition to the king along the same lines, and, as a result, on October 23, 1667, King Charles signed an order providing "that a temporary permission of seven yeares, with three shipps onely, be given and hereby granted unto the Dutch freely to trade with the Inhabitants of Lands lately reduced from the Dutch into the obedience of his Matie."[7]

The reactions of the British mercantile establishment during the twenty years following the metamorphosis of New Netherland into New York appear obscure and often contradictory. British merchants resolutely abstained from sending adequate supplies or trade goods to New York. Ritchie writes that in the years between 1664 and 1674, only two merchant vessels are recorded as sailing from the Port of London to New York.[8] There were, of course, other ports from which ships and cargoes could have cleared, and certainly some did, yet there is ample documentary evidence to support the claim that at this period British merchants, manufacturers, or shipping services—or perhaps all three—were not meeting the needs of the New York market.

Yet, throughout this period, despite their unwillingness or inability to satisfy the needs of the New Yorkers, the British merchants were actively trying through protests and pressures to force their government not to let the Dutch in Holland send ships, nor to allow the Dutch in New York to trade with Amsterdam. It was such a protest that caused the repeal of the king's order allowing Dutch ships to sail directly to New York with Dutch cargoes. An order in council of November 18, 1668, reads: ". . . the Council of Trade have represented to his Maty that the Merchants are much discouraged in their Trade to New Yorke . . . by reason of an indulgence granted to the Dutch . . . ," and as a result the king's order of October 23, 1667, was revoked.[9] Immediately, a group of merchants in New York countered with a complaint to the English government that if they could not bring their cargoes from Holland, their "wives and children would be ruined."[10]

A current historian of the New Netherland years believes that the ending of the West India Company's monopoly on trade with the Americas in 1638 gave to a group of Amsterdam merchants, among them the van Rensselaer family, an opportunity to develop an extremely successful trade during the New Netherland period. He concludes that the success of this powerful conclave of merchants, by siphoning the profits of the American trade into Amsterdam's coffers and thus deflecting them from those of New Netherland, may have been responsible for the commercial and financial "undoing" of that province.[11] That this may well be so is indicated by the reversal of roles that took place after 1664, when prominent Dutch-American merchants in New York City and Albany, free now from the powerful competition of Amsterdam but working against formidable legal obstacles thrown up by the British government, undertook a trade with Holland that would bring wealth to them and social and financial preeminence to their families for the next three hundred years.

One of the advantages enjoyed by these parvenu provincials was that they were not fastidious in business matters; they were unhampered by considerations of noblesse oblige or by the legal and ethical traditions that had governed the behavior of the old mercantile oligarchy of Amsterdam. Many of the New York Dutch had sprung from humble beginnings and had arrived at their present comfortable circumstances by seizing opportunities when they presented, often without allowing scruples to interfere with business. It could hardly be expected that they would now let international legalities come between themselves and a unique chance to make a great deal of money. They plunged into a situation that would tax all their economic ingenuity with the stubborn determination that had characterized the activities of Dutch traders for generations.

It is estimated by one writer on this subject that "fifty or so New York City or Albany merchants" engaged in the Amsterdam trade between 1666 and 1690. One way this trade was conducted was by smuggling, which, as we have seen, had been a way of life for the traders of New Netherland since the province was founded and continued to be in English New York. This writer points out that smuggling cargoes by way of New England or the New Jersey ports and establishing factors in foreign trade centers were important means by which New York merchants were able to carry on a profitable trade with Holland in the second half of the seventeenth century, and even later.[12] One English merchant, a man named Heathcote, was charged with illegal trading in Albany in 1676. In his testimony before the court he made the interesting statement that he could not sell his goods because there were so many cheap Dutch goods in Albany that had not cleared English ports.[13]

By the 1670s, British merchants were beginning to establish themselves in New York, and these were generally antagonistic to Governor Andros, who had a well-deserved reputation for favoring the interests of the Dutch merchants. With the removal of Andros in 1681 and his replacement with Thomas Dongan, who favored the English party, the economic situation changed. At this time the British economy was undergoing rapid changes as well and was beginning the climb toward a summit that in the following century would establish England as the world's foremost industrial and mercantile nation.

Although 1690, with the beginning of the series of wars with France that had such violent consequences for America, is generally taken as the approximate date when the balance of seaborne trade to America shifted from the Dutch to the English, the Dutch trade with New York did not in fact stop then. Matson says: "...although fewer merchants of Dutch origin traded to Amsterdam because English merchants and principles had 'invaded' New York City, even warfare did not obliterate the New York-Amsterdam trade. There were two to four registered voyages per year to Amsterdam from New York City from 1705 to 1716, and an uncertain number of illicit ones, which is generally the level at which New Yorkers traded to Amsterdam before 1689."[14]

Documents in New York City archives and in the New York State Library at Albany confirm that merchants of both cities traded with Amsterdam throughout the first half of the eighteenth century. Matson takes the trade up to 1764. Considering the amount of documentary evidence attesting to the extent and persistence of Dutch trade with America in our first century and a half, it is little short of incredible that the indexes of a great many books written in this century on the history of American trade do not show a listing for "Dutch."

1. Arnold J. F. van Laer, ed. and trans., *Documents Relating to New Netherland, 1624-1626* (San Marino, Calif.: Henry E. Huntington Library and Art Gallery, 1924), 228-29, 231.

2. Edmund B. O'Callaghan, *Documents Relative to the Colonial History of the State of New York* (Albany: Weed, Parsons and Co., 1853-1858), 3:163-64.

3. Robert C. Ritchie, "London Merchants, the New York Market, and the Recall of Sir Edmund Andros," *New York History* 57 (1976): 5-29.

4. Jan Kupp, "Aspects of New York-Dutch Trade under the English, 1670-1674," *New-York Historical Society Quarterly* 58 (1974): 139-41.

5. O'Callaghan, *Colonial History of the State of New York*, 3:163.

6. Ibid., 163-64.

7. Ibid., 166-67.

8. Ritchie, "London Merchants," 18.

9. O'Callaghan, *Colonial History of the State of New York*, 3:177.

10. Ibid.

11. Oliver Rink, "New Netherland and the Amsterdam Merchants: Unraveling a Secret Colonialism," *de Halve Maen* 59 (4), forthcoming.

12. Cathy Matson, "Commerce after the Conquest: Dutch Traders and Goods in New York City," *de Halve Maen* 59 (4), forthcoming.

13. Ritchie, "London Merchants," 22.

14. Matson, "Commerce after the Conquest."

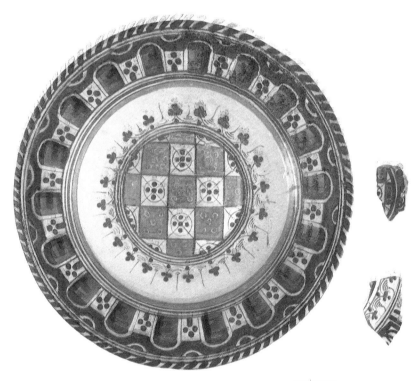

Above:
Plate 1. Dutch majolica plate, first half of the seventeenth century. This design was popular in Holland in the 1640s. Matching sherds from Fort Orange.
(Dishes) *Albany Institute of History and Art*
(Sherds) *New York State Office of Parks, Recreation and Historic Preservation*

Below:
Plate 2. Dutch majolica dish, first half of the seventeenth century. The gadrooned border shown here became popular in the late sixteenth century, as did the checkerboard (*shaakbord*) center design. Sherds from Fort Orange.
(Dishes) *Albany Institute of History and Art*
(Sherds) *New York State Office of Parks, Recreation and Historic Preservation*

Above:
Plate 3. Dutch majolica bowl with pomegranate, grape and leaf design, first half of the seventeenth century. Sherds from Fort Orange.
(Dishes) *Albany Institute of History and Art*
(Sherds) *New York State Office of Parks, Recreation and Historic Preservation*

Below:
Plate 4. Lead-glazed redware Dutch colander, seventeenth century. Sherd from Fort Orange.
(Dishes) *Albany Institute of History and Art*
(Sherds) *New York State Office of Parks, Recreation and Historic Preservation*

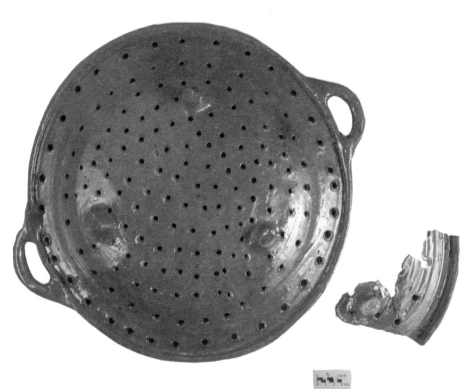

Above:
Plate 5. Dutch proto-fayence small bowl, first half of the seventeenth century. The design of this bowl from Fort Orange derives from Ming porcelain.
New York State Office of Parks, Recreation and Historic Preservation.

Below:
Plate 6. Dutch fayence plate, third quarter of the seventeenth century.
New York State Office of Parks, Recreation and Historic Preservation.

Above:
Plate 7. Dutch majolica sherds from Fort Orange showing both Italian and Chinese influences, first half of the seventeenth century.
New York State Office of Parks, Recreation and Historic Preservation.

Below:
Plate 8. Reverse of Dutch majolica sherds showing typical foot-rings, first half of the seventeenth century.
New York State Office of Parks, Recreation and Historic Preservation.

Above:
Plate 9. German stoneware from Fort Orange, first half of the
seventeenth century.
*New York State Office of Parks, Recreation and Historic
Preservation.*

Below:
Plate 10. Sherds of Bartmann jugs from Dutch sites such as Fort
Orange, with typical Frechen medallions, first half of the
seventeenth century.
*New York State Office of Parks, Recreation and Historic
Preservation.*

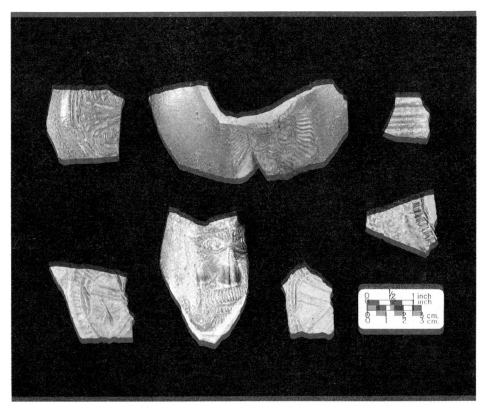

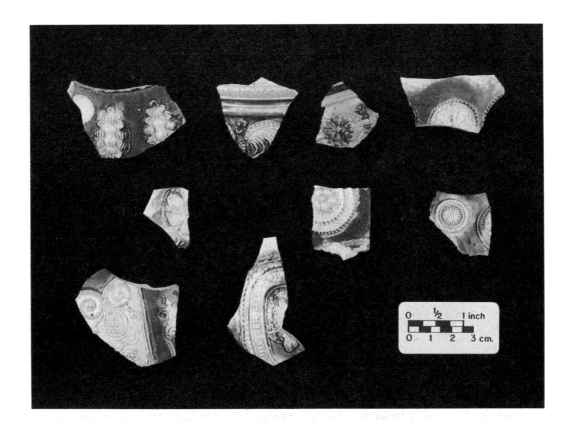

Above:
Plate 11. Westerwald stoneware sherds from Fort Orange, first half of the seventeenth century.
New York State Office of Parks, Recreation and Historic Preservation.

Below:
Plate 12. Dutch fayence sherds from Fort Orange, seventeenth century. Some of these have designs taken from Ming porcelain of the Wan-li period, others have Italian motifs.
New York State Office of Parks, Recreation and Historic Preservation.

Above:
Plate 13. Typical Dutch redware cooking pot from Fort Orange, first half of the seventeenth century. ht. 4 inches, rim dia. 4⅜ inches.
New York State Office of Parks, Recreation and Historic Preservation.

Below:
Plate 14. Sherds including skillet handle and fragments of a colander and a large shallow utility dish from Fort Orange, first half of the seventeenth century.
New York State Office of Parks, Recreation and Historic Preservation.

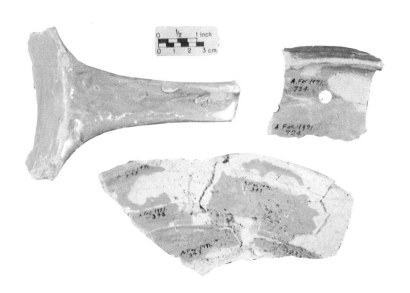

Above:
Plate 15. Dutch utility ware similar to types found at Fort Orange, seventeenth century.
Albany Institute of History and Art

Below:
Plate 16. Dutch utility earthenware similar to that recovered at Fort Orange, seventeenth century.
Albany Institute of History and Art

10
Dutch Trade with the Later Colonies and Florida

Since Pennsylvania and the Carolinas were settled by the English relatively late in the seventeenth century, and for the most part after the Dutch political presence in America had ended, they have not claimed a large space in this study. Yet in view of the persistence and success of the Dutch in trading with the other English colonies in spite of legal obstacles, it is unreasonable to suppose that there was no Dutch trade with these three colonies.

Since Pennsylvania was settled by the Quakers, with whom the Dutch had previously established good trade relations in Rhode Island, it seems likely that the latter traded with the Philadelphia merchants, particularly in the early years of the proprietary government there. Both Carolinas were settled after the New Netherland period and thus were not involved in trade with the Dutch such as the earlier-founded English colonies had maintained. Nor has there been in recent years sufficient archaeological exploration on seventeenth-century sites in those two states to produce a comprehensive record. Nevertheless, it may be presumed that some of the raw products of the Carolinas—pitch, tar, tobacco, rice, and lumber—constituted a part of the Dutch Atlantic trade.

That such a trade was feasible for them is suggested by a passage in a nineteenth-century history of South Carolina. This refers to the Dutch nation in a legal decision on trade made by South Carolina officials in the seventeenth century based on the not entirely convincing reasoning that since the proprietary government of 1670-1719 had been founded subsequent to the passage of the Navigation Acts, it was not subject to their restraints. As a result, these acts were "disregarded and They traded as they pleased."[1]

Florida, long the property of Spain, probably maintained a trading connection with the Dutch throughout the seventeenth century. Neither the Dutch nor the Spanish had ever allowed enmity or even actual war to interfere unduly in their trading with each other.

The established Dutch image as the most enterprising trading nation in Europe during the seventeenth century, the extent of the documentation attesting to the Dutch trade with the English colonies in America at that time, and the wealth of evidence that neither the colonists nor the Dutch had any fastidious scruples against smuggling, all support the probability that the Dutch trade with America was far more extensive than was earlier recognized.

There is likewise abundant documentary testimony to establish that by the early years of the seventeenth century the Dutch had acquired a great deal of experience in coordinating manufactures and shipping into a highly effective mercantile hegemony. England, on the other hand, was still basically an agricultural society during the first half of the seventeenth century, and was engaged for part of that time in a devastating civil war that taxed all her energies. In those years she lacked the ships, the sailors, and the economic organizational experience needed to supply her colonies with the quantity and quality of consumer goods that recent archaeological recoveries on those sites show they enjoyed. Thus, these artifacts can no longer be presumed, as they once were, to have arrived here solely through the means of English distribution.

Perhaps the reason that some historians and archaeologists have difficulty accepting this is that in the past many American historians have suggested that the English Navigation Acts were held sacrosanct by one and all, ignoring the fact that the Dutch had flouted these laws from their inception. Indeed, it was not until the last quarter of the seventeenth century, when England replaced the Netherlands as the leading maritime power, that she could seriously challenge Dutch circumvention of English maritime statutes. Even so, the Dutch continued to trade with America well into the eighteenth century.

Notes - Chapter 10

1. Edward McCrady, *History of South Carolina under the Proprietary Government, 1670-1719* (New York: Macmillan and Co., 1897), 213.

PART II
CERAMICS

11
Seventeenth-Century Dutch Ceramics

During the last quarter of the nineteenth century, Henry Havard wrote a book that propelled seventeenth-century Dutch fayence (delft) into the international ceramics limelight.[1] Suddenly, many Americans of Dutch ancestry began to look upon this ware as a kind of clan totem, and some who could afford it even made pilgrimages to Holland to buy Dutch fayence. At the same time, other, much earlier Dutch ceramics went unnoticed by collectors in America and even in the Netherlands.

Within the last eighty years, archaeologists in the Netherlands have rediscovered these earlier wares and have understood their value as significant cultural material. Even more recently, American archaeologists have established to their surprise that these same types of Dutch ceramics were used widely in America in the colonial period. Thus, on both sides of the Atlantic a new interest has arisen in all Dutch seventeenth-century ceramics that transcends the interest that formerly surrounded Dutch fayence. This has motivated archaeologists and antiquarians in both countries to cooperate in research on the incidence of Dutch wares on seventeenth-century American settlement sites and on the avenues of trade by which they arrived here. It has also increased the need for published information in the English language about these questions.

In the dark ages that followed the Roman withdrawal from northern Europe and the British Isles, whatever sophisticated ceramic techniques the conquerors had introduced into those parts were largely forgotten, and eventually the local wares degenerated into dark-colored, lead-glazed utility wares. Only the red-bodied floor tiles, their use confined for the most part to religious houses, had much claim to aesthetic superiority. Although these employed only earth colors, many were skillfully decorated with intricate incised designs in contrasting slips.

By the fifteenth century, the quality of northern European lead-glazed earthenwares had improved, and they had become more diverse in shapes and colors. The potters of the German Rhineland led in the production of these new utility wares, and Hol-land, through its trading operations along the Rhine River, was, for a time, the prime market for them. But the Dutch, never ones to pass up an economic opportunity, eventually began the manufacture of their own utility wares, fabricating these along much the same lines as those they had been importing for so long from Germany. Strangely, it is only within recent years, through the discoveries of Dutch archaeologists, that certain types of lead-glazed earthenware previously thought to be of German manufacture have been recognized as Dutch in origin. A useful record of these Dutch utility wares that were used in the taverns, the kitchens of the wealthy, and the homes of the less affluent is preserved in Dutch seventeenth-century drawings and *genre* paintings and in the artifacts recovered through modern Dutch archaeology. These constitute visual and documentary evidence difficult to question.

Another important development in the production of fine ceramics in Europe occurred around the middle of the sixteenth century with the manufacture in the Netherlands of majolica, a tin-glazed earthenware that received its whiteness from the use of tin oxide as an opacifier. Although in the sixteenth century the Dutch were deeply involved in the war with Spain, their urban centers had not been so decimated by it as had those in the Spanish Netherlands (Belgium) to the south. The majolica industry, newly transplanted from the south, thrived in Holland in a number of places, among these the city of Haarlem. During the first half of the seventeenth century, this city, one of the most active pottery centers in the Netherlands because of its proximity to Amsterdam, may have furnished much of the majolica shipped to America.

Majolica was the prototype of the later and vastly more celebrated Dutch fayence that is now popularly known as "delft," the Dutch manufacture of which resulted from the introduction into Holland of Chinese porcelain. This Far Eastern novelty found instant favor with the Dutch wealthy classes but was too expensive for the average householder. Dutch potters shrewdly decided that they could open up an entirely new market by copying the Chinese product in a tin-glazed earthenware that was finer, thinner, and whiter than the old majolica and decorating it in blue Chinese designs. As usual, the Dutch entrepreneurial instinct was correct, and the new ware proved a great commercial success. A prominent and experienced Dutch archaeologist believes that the manufacture of fayence in Holland was not well established until around 1640.[2]

Beginning in the nineteenth century, probably as a result of Havard's ambitious work, the word *Delft* established itself as a generic name for all tin-glazed earthenware of Dutch or English provenance. Even though many persons writing within this area of ceramic research found it inadequate since the city of Delft represented only one source of this type of pottery, the word continued to be used—often with a lower-case *d*. Among those apparently committed to this usage have been American archaeologists, many of whom even appear to resist the use of the term *majolica* to distinguish the earlier type of Dutch and English tin-glazed earthenware.

Today some archaeologists and museum personnel in the Netherlands are discontinuing use of the term *Delft* except in connection with wares known to have originated in that city. J. D. van Dam, curator of the Princessehof Museum in Leeuwarden, Friesland, and a Dutch authority on tin-glazed wares, employed the words *majolica* and *fayence* in an article to distinguish between the early Dutch ware with a staniferous glaze on only the obverse side and its successor, the more sophisticated ware with a tin glaze on both surfaces.[3] The term *Delft* was reserved for pieces made in the factories of that city. This breakthrough in ceramic nomenclature is sensible and will be followed in this book. On the other hand, English tin-glazed earthenware will be designated either as English majolica or English delftware, depending on whether it has a lead or tin glaze on the reverse. This decision may seem inconsistent but may be defended on pragmatic grounds—or so we believe.

During the transitional period between the exclusive manufacture of majolica and the early years of fayence production (roughly 1629-1669), much of the latter ware had certain qualities of both products. Such pieces are now sometimes referred to as proto-delft or, more properly, proto-fayence.

Before the seventeenth century, Dutch traders had distributed Dutch majolica and utility wares, as well as Rhenish stonewares and even Italian artifacts, to the British Isles and to various parts of Europe, including Russia[4] and the Scandinavian countries.[5] By the first quarter of the seventeenth century, the Dutch were establishing themselves as an economic and political power in America and were cruising and trading the length of our eastern seaboard, in the course of which they again distributed ceramic products in trade.

Although at this time the Netherlands was developing a ceramics industry designed to compete with any in Europe, ceramics were not a principal commodity in the Dutch trade with America, as they were at that time in Dutch commerce with the Orient, or as they would be for England in the eighteenth century. The trade of the Dutch, as discussed in Part I, depended primarily on such commodities as furs, tobacco, tar, lumber, grain, textiles, fish, wine, rum, sugar, and slaves. Ceramics were merely a kind of *leitmotif*, always there. Yet today, the greater products have turned to dust, while the Dutch ceramics endure, their glazes as undulled, their colors as undimmed as on the day they were put ashore. It is these that provide material evidence of the extent of Dutch trade in America in the seventeenth century.

Notes - Chapter 11

1. Henry Havard, *Histoire de la faïence de Delft* (Paris: E. Plon et Cie., 1878), 1:51.
2. Personal communication with Jan Baart.
3. J. D. van Dam, "Geleyersgoet en Hollants porceleyn: Ontwikkelingen in de Nederlandse aardewerk-industrie, 1560-1660," *Mededelingenblad, Nederlandse vereniging van vrienden van de ceramiek* 108 (1982/84): 88.
4. Conversation held in May 1980 with Pieter Jan Tichelaar, director of a famous pottery factory in Makkum, Friesland, that was shipping ceramics to Russia in the seventeenth century; also, Juhani Gronhagen, "Underwater Archaeology in Finland" (Paper read at meeting of the Society for Historical Archaeology, Boston, January 1985).
5. When the Swedish warship, *Wasa*, which sank at its launching in 1628, was brought to the surface in recent years, Dutch majolica and utility wares were found on board.

12
Dutch Utility Wares

Obscurity often surrounds the more utilitarian objects of any past culture since these are usually considered too commonplace to preserve beyond the point of their usefulness. Yet such artifacts are closest to the core of the home and have pertinence in determining the socioeconomic status of the people who used them. Although these earthen vessels of the past have survived in scores of Dutch *genre* paintings, until lately few had made their way into museums. Fortunately, Dutch archaeology now recognizes their cultural significance and is concerned for their recovery and preservation.

But while today it is easy enough to learn what the Dutch utility wares of three hundred years ago looked like (Pls. 4, 13-16; Fig. 4), their provenance and the history of their manufacture are far more difficult to sort out than are those of the more sophisticated tin-glazed earthenwares or the Rhenish stonewares. This puzzle is complicated not only by the persistent trade the Dutch carried on with England, Ireland, and Germany over several centuries prior to the seventeenth, but also by the industrial rivalry that prompted at least three of these nations to copy the ceramic products of the others.

To what extent redwares indistinguishable in composition and appearance from the German Werra and Wanfried wares (see chapter 15) were being made in the Netherlands in the seventeenth century is a question that today occupies the interest and investigations of Dutch archaeologists. In the 1960s, redwares startlingly similar to Wanfried ware—many of the pieces, like their German counterparts, bearing inscribed dates—were discovered in such concentrated quantities in several places in the province of North Holland as to suggest that they had been manufactured there (Fig. 4).[1] Because kiln sites have not been located in that region, however, and since it is an area that was convenient to the early shipping lanes from the Rhineland, current opinion is divided as to whether these artifacts were made in North Holland or in Germany.[2]

There appears to be no room for doubt, however, that kilns discovered in the 1970s in the province of

Utrecht, in the central part of the Netherlands, were producing red-bodied slipwares similar to the German wares as early as the fifteenth century. By the

Fig. 4. "North Holland" slip-decorated redware sherds, seventeenth century. These sherds found at Fort Orange represent a type of Dutch-made utility ware inspired by earlier redware types imported by the Dutch from Germany.
New York State Office of Parks, Recreation and Historic Preservation

sixteenth century, favorite designs appearing on these redware dishes were linked arcs in trailed slip and *sgraffito* patterns.[3] The manufacture of pottery with such designs apparently continued into the seventeenth century.

Throughout that century, a simpler type of lead-glazed redware was being made in Holland, probably in many different localities. This was an undecorated ware, cinnamon brown in color and often having minute dark brown flecks in the shiny lead glaze. It was undoubtedly the plainest and cheapest of the Dutch-made earthenwares in the seventeenth century and was used universally in New Netherland. A type of earthenware similiar to this Dutch redware was made in England in the seventeenth century,[4] as well as in Virginia.

Red-bodied and buff-bodied wares were not the only utility ceramics being manufactured in the

Netherlands in the seventeenth century, however. As early as the twelfth century, earthenware with a grainy white body decorated with a yellow and green glaze was being made in the Southern Netherlands, near Liège (Belgium). In the sixteenth century this manufacture moved northward into Flanders, and thence into Holland[5]—a progression later duplicated by majolica. Kiln wasters from Haarlem and Utrecht indicate that this kind of white-bodied ware was being made in those cities as early as the fourteenth century,[6] and it is known that the Dutch were distributing earthenware of this kind in trade with other countries, especially to the East Anglia area of England, in the late sixteenth and seventeenth centuries.[7] This white-bodied ware of the Dutch was made in green or yellow, or with the two colors combined on the same vessel, usually with the yellow glaze inside, and often with the glaze carelessly applied to the outer side.

There is much confusion between this Dutch green-and-yellow earthenware and a similar type said to have been made in England along the Hampshire-Surrey border as early as the sixteenth century.[8] An example of this pottery is mentioned in Henry Miller's report as being found in the Leonard Calvert house in St. Mary's City.[9] Since early Dutch ceramics were found in the same context, however, it is equally possible that the Calvert house sherd is of Dutch, not English, manufacture. These tangled lines of provenance for utility earthenwares are not simply minutiae of no consequence, but rather have substantial importance in determining Dutch trade patterns in colonial America.

Three distinct varieties of lead-glazed green wares have been found on seventeenth-century sites in the area formerly known as New Netherland: one with a forest green glaze and a coarse white body, the previously mentioned light green combined with yellow, and one with a brilliant green glaze and a fine-grained, dark red body that appears to have a thin, white slip between body and glaze. The green Dutch wares were made in many different utility forms, including bowls, pipkins, colanders and small jugs (Pls. 4, 13-16). There are also thick, square floor tiles in green that have a coarse red body, a white slip separating it from the glaze. Similar brown-glazed floor tiles are also common on New Netherland sites.

Printed information in English on seventeenth-century Dutch utility wares and their distribution falls far short of that available for the tin-glazed wares. Of late, however, interest in this aspect of Dutch ceramics has widened, and more is being published about it in Holland and England. Today, the best sources for this are: (1) papers written by Dutch, English, and American archaeologists for professional publications and (2) museum publications and catalogs of exhibits of these wares. An excellent example of the latter is that entitled *Van huisvuil tot museumstuk* (From household rubbish to museum pieces), published in 1981 by the Nijmeegs Museum Commanderie van Sint Jan. This contains fine photographs and gives helpful details about a number of utility forms recovered in the city of Nijmegen, Gelderland, during archaeological excavations there. The brochure published by the Fries Museum, Leeuwarden, Friesland, entitled *Vondsten uit eigen bodem* (Discoveries from our own ground), has a section describing utility wares discovered in 1978, during construction of a new wing for the museum. The Fries Museum is located almost directly across the street from the former Chancellery of the Emperor Charles V, and is thus in one of the oldest parts of the city of Leeuwarden.

With the exception of a short English summary of a booklet by J. G. N. Renaud entitled *Rhodesteyn, schatkamer der middeleeuwse ceramiek*, describing the Van Beuningen collection in the small museum at Rhodesteyn, Neerlangbroek (province of Utrecht), and several articles in British archaeological publications, there is almost nothing available in English on these Dutch utility wares. A catalog of an exhibit and symposium held at the Museum Boymans-van Beuningen in Rotterdam in the spring of 1973, entitled *Verdraaid goed gedraaid*, shows excellent photographs that are of help in understanding this ware that archaeologists have found in quantity on seventeenth-century Dutch sites in America. A book in English would be of great help. Perhaps the best collection of Dutch utility wares is that assembled by H. J. E. van Beuningen of the Netherlands.

Notes - Chapter 12

1. John G. Hurst, D. S. Neal, and H. J. E. van Beuningen, "North Holland Slipware," in *Rotterdam Papers* 2 (Rotterdam: J. G. N. Renaud, 1975), 47.
2. This was called to my attention by Paul R. Huey.
3. Hurst, Neal, and van Beuningen, "North Holland Slipware," 49.
4. "Continental Post-Medieval Wares," *East Anglian Archaeology,* Report 13 (1981): 136.
5. J. R. A. M. Thijssen, "Gebruiksaardewerk met loodglazur," in *Van huisvuil tot museumstuk* (Nijmegen: Nijmeegs Museum Commanderie van Sint Jan, 1981), 9.
6. Ibid.
7. "Continental Post-Medieval Wares," 134.
8. F. Holling, "Reflections on Tudor Green," *Post-Medieval Archaeology* 11 (1977): 61, 63.
9. Henry M. Miller, *A Search for the "Citty of Saint Maries,"* St. Mary's City Archaeology Series, no. 1 (St. Mary's City, Md.: St. Mary's City Commission, 1983), 51.

Around the middle of the sixteenth century, Italian potters who had been working in Antwerp introduced the manufacture of tin-glazed earthenware, known as majolica, into the Northern Netherlands. This represented the first white-glazed ware ever used in this northern region with the exception of the fine white salt-glazed *Krüge* made at Siegburg in the previous century. In actuality, the majolica was white only on its upper or obverse side, with a lead glaze on the reverse side.

This Dutch majolica is a vividly colored, rather thick, and heavily decorated ware, and it was used universally in Dutch households during the later sixteenth and first half of the seventeenth centuries (Pls. 1, 2, 3, 7, 8; Figs. 7-17, 27, 28, 29). Representations of it occur in a number of Dutch *genre* paintings of the time (Fig. 5), and therefore it seems all the more strange that by the twentieth century this early majolica had been all but forgotten by the Dutch themselves. This was doubtless because it had been displaced by another, much finer type of tin-glazed ceramic, fayence, and thus had early ceased to be thought of as a ware to be preserved.

Fig. 5. Detail from **Kitchen Interior**, by Willem Kalf (1619-1693), showing broken Dutch majolica dish of a pattern found at Fort Orange.
Saint Louis Art Museum, Saint Louis, Missouri

Tin-glazed earthenware, one of the few fine ceramic types that owes no debt to the Chinese, is believed to have had its origin in Mesopotamia around the ninth century. From there it quickly spread throughout the Islamic world and was eventually introduced into western Europe by Spain's Moorish conquerors. Drawing inspiration and techniques from its Middle Eastern prototype, Spanish tin-glazed pottery developed into the lustred Hispano-Moresque ware that reached its peak in the fifteenth century.

ITALIAN *MAIOLICA*, PROTOTYPE OF DUTCH MAJOLICA

It has long been assumed and often stated that Hispano-Moresque lustrewares were introduced into Italy in the course of that country's trade with the Balearic Islands, and that the Italian word *maiolica* derives from Majorca, one of those islands from which the Spanish lustreware was obtained. In recent years, there has been a tendency to question this derivation. In any case, however much the Spanish lustres may have influenced Italian *maiolica* of the High Renaissance, there is increasing evidence that non-lustred tin-glazed earthenware having no connection with Spain was being made in Italy as early as the first quarter of the thirteenth century.[1]

Later Italian potters were inspired by the Spanish lustre techniques and set about copying them, but instead of restricting themselves to the gold lustre and dark blue of the Spanish prototype, they were soon producing more vigorous decorations in a palette that included purple, green, blue, and an orange-yellow made from iron rust.

Cipriano Piccolpasso, an Italian who, in the mid-sixteenth century, wrote the first comprehensive treatise on the art of making *maiolica*, tells us that these colors were later extended to include a lemon yellow, made from antimony; a white pigment called *bianchetto*, used for the *bianco sopra bianco* type of decoration;[2] a blue-tinted enamel; and a black made by combining copper, manganese, and *zaffre* (a form of cobalt) with sand and lead. He also describes a red peculiar to the potters of Faenza that was achieved by painting over light yellow with Armenian bole (an ochreous clay) ground with red vinegar.[3] It would appear that the Italians learned this technique for making a brilliant red from Turkish potters, who employed it in the fifteenth century on Isnik pottery.

Eventually, Italian potters produced far more colorful lustrewares than those of Spain, but it was not these, nor the famed *istoriato* of the High Renaissance,[4] that they later took to the Netherlands, but, instead, a simpler tin-glazed type of earthenware that took its essence from much earlier Italian tin-glazed earthenware. This latter product, decorated in polychrome or sometimes in blue and white, was the prototype for Dutch and English majolica wares for the next hundred years. It is impossible to overemphasize the degree to which these were influenced by the Italian decorative designs.

During the early sixteenth century, many Italian potters moved northward with their craft, often heading for Antwerp, then the center of northern European culture. We learn from the writings of Piccolpasso that at this time Guido da Savino, a potter from Castel Durante (one of the great Italian centers for making *maiolica*), carried the art to Antwerp and was joined there by other Italian craftsmen.

In the second half of the sixteenth century, however, politico-religious strife between the Southern Netherlands and Spain made the climate of Antwerp unfavorable to commerce or the development of new industries. As a result, Italian potters whose fathers had settled in that city began to leave, some going to England,[5] others to the Northern Netherlands. From this, the pottery industry of Antwerp suffered a reverse from which it never recovered.

DUTCH MAJOLICA

Joris Andries, son of Guido da Savino, went to Middelburg, in Zeeland, in 1564, where he established a pottery. This city was one of the first in the Northern Netherlands in which majolica was made, and apparently other potters were there around the time Joris Andries arrived. There were also potteries in Amsterdam, Haarlem, and Rotterdam. By the end of the sixteenth century, majolica manufactories existed in a number of towns in the Northern Netherlands.

It is now known through archaeological work in Amsterdam that many years before Italian potters arrived in the Low Countries, *maiolica* from Italy was being imported into Holland. This whole question is clarified in a paper given by Jan Baart, archaeologist of the city of Amsterdam, at a ceramics conference in Italy in 1983. According to Baart, "earthenware identified with certainty as Italian appears for the first time in a group of discoveries dated 1475-1500." He then describes the decoration of several early dishes that suggests they came from a location near Florence, probably Montelupo, but says that the real basis for identification of these as Italian and from that general area is their fine clay.[6]

Speaking of the meticulous imitations of Italian *maiolica* that gradually came to be made by Dutch potters, Baart says that the painters of the decoration followed "as in the case of the checkerboard motif" (Pl. 2) the patterns of Montelupo examples, interpreting them, however, in their own way, and sometimes using an Italian decoration on the rim of a dish with a representation of their own choosing in the center.[7]

The first Dutch majolica was made in the same way and with many of the same patterns as its Italian prototype, utilizing the procedures and colors described by Piccolpasso. The first potter of majolica mentioned in the archives of Amsterdam was an immigrant, Carstiaen van den Abeele, who arrived there from Bruges before 1581. In Bergen op Zoom, however, the first majolica potters are mentioned in the archives of the early decades of the sixteenth century.[8]

In an article in *Oud Holland*, written in 1926, Ferrand Hudig states that seventeenth-century Dutch documents refer to this Dutch majolica sometimes as *Straats goed* (Straits ware) and sometimes as *wit goed* (white ware).[9] The first of these names derives from the Straits of Gibraltar, through which the Italian majolica had first reached the Netherlands; the second refers to a product with a white surface, as opposed to the older Dutch redwares that it displaced.

Shortly after 1600, Chinese porcelain began to be imported into Holland in increasing quantities, and this fine ware became extremely popular with the Dutch. Their potters soon began to capitalize on its popularity by developing a tin-glazed earthenware decorated in Chinese motifs which was difficult to distinguish from the porcelain without close examination. Together, this ware, which we now call fayence (delft), and the porcelain were to destroy the majolica industry in the Netherlands, except in Friesland, where it took hold strongly in the second half of the seventeenth century and flourished for the next 150 years.[10]

Familiarity with the previously mentioned article by Hudig is almost essential to an understanding of the dichotomy between majolica and fayence and the shift from the former to the latter. In his article, unfortunately available only in Dutch, Hudig describes a lawsuit between two Haarlem potters, a father and son, that stemmed from this transformation in the potting industry of Holland during the mid-seventeenth century.[11]

Willem Jansz Verstraeten, *alias* De Rue, the father, was established as an important potter prior to 1625. In 1642, he sold his pottery to his son, Gerrit Willemsz, and set up a new business for himself in the Spaarne (an area of Haarlem). Under the agreement made at that time, the father, referred to in the documents as a *plateelbakker* (majolica-maker), would confine his production to the old-style majolica, while the son, called a *Hollants porceleynbakker* ("Hollants porceleyn" was not porcelain but fayence), would have the right to manufacture only the new ware—fayence.[12] After a time, the father became dissatisfied with the arrangement, possibly because the public flocked to buy the new product, neglecting the old, and a long series of legal actions between the two men began.

The father accused his son of making certain forms and patterns forbidden to him by the original contract. The two products most prominent in the record of the litigation are armorial ware (*wapengoed*) and small bowls (Fig. 6) called *clapmutsen* by the Dutch. The father contended that he had an exclusive right to manufacture these since they belonged in the province of the majolica-makers. This suit, which dragged on for some years, is valuable for showing that the distinction made today between majolica and fayence was recognized as valid and important in the seventeenth century as well.

Fig. 6. Detail from **Still Life with Lobster**, by Johannes Hannot (1633-1685), shows small Chinese Ming bowl that is the prototype of certain seventeenth-century Dutch fayence bowls called *clapmutsen*, one of which was found at Fort Orange. (See Plate 5.) *Private Owner*

The Dutch majolica industry in Holland did not die all at once, however. It slipped away gradually between 1640 and 1670 as the demand for the new product, which was lighter colored with a finer-grained body and white enamel on all surfaces, made it obsolete. After a time, the manufacture of majolica was confined to Friesland. There, notably in Makkum, Bolsward, and Harlingen, a vigorous folk product continued to be made. This largely ignored Italian and Chinese motifs in favor of Dutch designs. A color combination particularly popular was blue and manganese, part of the design often being applied with a sponge—characteristics sometimes used as criteria for identifying Frisian majolica.

BODY AND APPEARANCE

The coarse earthenware body of Dutch majolica varied slightly in color from period to period and firing to firing, encompassing shades of salmon pink, gray, tan, and buff. Potters were using the native, red-firing clays of the Northern Netherlands to make tiles, slipwares, and utilitarian wares there even before majolica was introduced. Although firing temperature affects body color somewhat, in Dutch majolica a red or gray body usually indicates an earlier period of manufacture. The reddish body of certain majolica plates dating from the 1630s and 1640s, however, suggests that even at that period dishes of a poorer quality were still being made from the local clays.

The sources from which the Dutch received their clay supplies at various periods appear to have been strongly influenced by the exigencies of war. In the late sixteenth century, while the Dutch were at war with Spain, which occupied the Southern Netherlands (now Belgium), clay from Doornik (Tournai) became unobtainable, and the Dutch began importing English clay for use in the potteries. This chalky clay, when mixed with local clays, produced a light yellow body similar to that of the later fayence. In 1609 a truce with Spain was declared, and Flemish clays from Doornik were once more available to the Dutch. When the truce ended in 1621, however, the Dutch again turned to the English, who appear to have supplied clay for the Dutch potteries until the beginning of the Anglo-Dutch wars in the mid-seventeenth century.[13,14]

The body of Dutch majolica is characteristically thick, on some large dishes reaching one-half inch near the footring. Outer rims are likewise thick, though sometimes thinner in pieces made around the middle of the seventeenth century, when both the fayence of Delft and Chinese porcelain had established a precedent for delicate lines.

The lead-glazed undersides of majolica dishes (Pl. 8) vary in appearance from piece to piece, in a range of at least three different color tones: a clear lead glaze laid directly on the unfired body and taking its color from that, a light gray glaze shading into gray-green with turquoise tints, and a cream-colored glaze. In the case of the two latter variations, there is the appearance of a thin slip or *engobe* underneath, a characteristic which Brigitte Tietzel mentions in her catalog of majolica in the museum at Cologne.[15] This appearance of a slip on the back of majolica dishes may be brought about by the addition to the lead glaze of factory waste containing a modicum of tin.

The varying greenish tones in the glaze of certain dishes probably derive from impurities in the glazing materials. Though the green shade may have been accomplished deliberately, it seems unlikely. Generally speaking, the earlier majolica dishes have a transparent lead glaze on their backs, with the green or cream tone appearing somewhat later.

Footrings are customary on Dutch majolica plates and dishes, and are low and flat, though often as wide as three-quarters of an inch, and usually unglazed or scantily glazed on their bottom edge. Even on small dishes, footrings were usually pierced for hanging at the time of manufacture, frequently with curiously little regard for the orientation of the design (Fig. 27).

Marks occur only occasionally on Dutch majolica and apparently were used more in the early years of its manufacture than later. They can rarely be identified. Testimony in the Verstraeten case shows that Willem Jansz, the father, used marks, but Hudig's article does not disclose what they looked like.

Sometimes dates occur on dishes and tiles, and these are usually accepted as being contemporary with manufacture, though in some instances this is questionable.

TECHNIQUES OF MANUFACTURE

As previously noted, the method the Dutch used for making the tin glaze for majolica differed little from that set forth by Piccolpasso. Sand and a potash derived from calcined wine lees[16] were melted together to form a frit,[17] called *marzacotto* by the Italians. Thirty parts of this frit and twelve parts of a lead- and tin-oxide mixture, in which there were approximately three parts of lead to one of tin, were then melted together to make the white tin glaze in which both whiteness and opacity were contributed by the tin.[18] Once this fusion hardened, it was ground fine, suspended in water, and the resulting liquid brushed or poured onto the principal or top surface of the vessel to be glazed, which had previously been fired at a relatively low temperature. This glaze,

Fig. 7. Dutch majolica polychrome plate in geometric design, first half of the seventeenth century, with matching sherd from Fort Orange. Note prominent *proen* marks.
(Plate) *Albany Institute of History and Art*
(Sherd and photo) *New York State Office of Parks, Recreation and Historic Preservation*

Fig. 8. *Left*, reverse side of Dutch fayence saucer showing three equidistant unglazed saggar marks along the underrim; *above right*, Dutch majolica sherd showing an unglazed spot that is a *proen* mark on the obverse side; *bottom*, a *proen* found archaeologically in Holland and lacking its upward-extending prongs. *Private Owner*

when dry, formed a powdery white surface on which designs could be painted in colors. The piece was finally refired at a temperature high enough to fix the colors and fuse the glaze. Unlike Dutch fayence, Dutch majolica was rarely given the second lead glaze that the Dutch called *kwaart*.

Dutch majolica was not fired in saggars[19] but was placed in the open kiln on small supports, or, in the case of plates and dishes, stacked upside down with triangular supports called *proenen* inserted between them to prevent fusion (Figs. 7, 8). These supports, when broken away at the end of the firing, left three unglazed spots in a triangular pattern on the obverse of the plate. These, along with other characteristics, serve to distinguish majolica from fayence, which has three equidistant narrow scars along the under rims of plates and large dishes caused by saggar supports (Fig. 8).

Majolica was fired at a temperature of between 900° and 1000° C.

DECORATION

Dutch majolica originally took its decorative inspiration almost exclusively from Italian *maiolica*. Faenza probably contributed the most to its designs, though Deruta, Florence, Urbino and other pottery centers added their motifs as well.

There is a popular feathery design known as the *aigrette* border that was adopted from the *maiolica* of Faenza, and this is often, though by no means always, found in company with a *putto* as the center motif (Figs. 9, 10). The Dutch also call this the Haarlem border, although it is agreed that it was produced in other places in the Netherlands besides Haarlem. A folk name for the same design is *hanepooten met crabben*, freely translated, "cocksfeet with scratches."

Chinese influence on the decoration of majolica for a long time was represented only by one late Ming design that has come to be known as the Wan-li pattern—a dark-blue-paneled-rim border of stylized chrysanthemums and Chinese symbols (Figs. 11, 12, 28, 29). This was one of the most popular of all majolica designs and is found extensively on some seventeenth-century American sites today. Sometimes this border surrounds a central design that includes birds, flowers, insects, and large rocks in a Chinese garden setting; sometimes it is used with a central decoration of Dutch or Italian tradition, or with a portly Chinese figure standing within a gate in the foreground. It was not until the middle of the seventeenth century, after the Delft influence had become very strong, that more diversified Chinese designs were employed on majolica.

Fig. 9. Dutch majolica dish, first half of the seventeenth century. The popular *aigrette* or Haarlem border shown here, with similar sherds from Fort Orange, derives from an Italian motif.
(Dish) *Albany Institute of History and Art*
(Sherds and photo) *New York State Office of Parks, Recreation and Historic Preservation*

Fig. 11. Dutch majolica bowl with Wan-li border and Chinese symbols also in the center, first half of the seventeenth century.
(Bowl) *Albany Institute of History and Art*
(Photo) *New York State Office of Parks, Recreation and Historic Preservation*

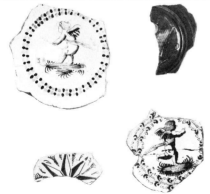

Fig. 10. Sherds of Dutch majolica polychrome dishes recovered in Amsterdam in 1931, with Italianate design elements also found on Fort Orange sherds, first half of the seventeenth century. The sherd at the upper right has a blue ground and derives from a type of Italian fayence known as *berettino* ware. (See Plate 7 for similar specimen from Fort Orange.)
Royal Dutch Antiquarian Society; on loan to the Rijksmuseum, Amsterdam, Holland

Fig. 12. Dutch majolica dish with Wan-li border and a center motif of a Chinese gentleman, first half of the seventeenth century. The matching sherds are from Fort Orange.
(Dish) *Albany Institute of History and Art*
(Sherds and photo) *New York State Office of Parks, Recreation and Historic Preservation*

In the sixteenth and early seventeenth centuries, strong, vivid colors covered much of the upper surface of a majolica dish or tile. Later, white areas expanded, and by the middle of the seventeenth century, this generous white ground was often decorated with scenes of Dutch life, Dutch buildings, flowers, and other evidences of Dutch taste. Border decorations, however, continued to follow the Italian or Chinese style.

Dutch specialists are reluctant to attribute designs exclusively to the potters of one city or another, holding that the majority of designs were common to all centers of manufacture, perhaps because the potters of the Netherlands, like most early potters, often moved about from place to place. One exception, however, is armorial ware or *wapengoed*, which is universally associated with the kilns of Haarlem. These dishes often bear the coat of arms of a municipal corporation, a military company, or a trade guild, and frequently both the arms and the foliated decoration surrounding them are applied in a careless, untidy manner.

Dingeman Korf states that in the second half of the sixteenth century the influence of the Flemish potters who had introduced majolica into the Northern Netherlands remained so pervasive that Dutch majolica made at that period is virtually indistinguishable from that of Flanders, but that by the beginning of the seventeenth century the Dutch were evolving a style of their own, more sober and restrained than the Flemish, and one that relied heavily on the geometric. Thus, he says, in spite of foreign influences on Dutch majolica, a unique Northern Netherlandish type came into being (Figs. 13, 14).[20]

Fig. 13. Dutch majolica plate, first quarter of the seventeenth century. This was a popular geometric pattern with Dutch majolica potters.
Private Owner

Fig. 14. Dutch majolica polychrome dish in star pattern with matching sherds from Fort Orange, first half of the seventeenth century.
(Dish) *Albany Institute of History and Art*
(Sherds and photo) *New York State Office of Parks, Recreation and Historic Preservation*

Several explanations may be suggested for the divergence of Dutch majolica from its prototype. By the beginning of the seventeenth century, Dutch potters and ceramic decorators, even those from Italian backgrounds, constituted a second generation much further removed from Italian aesthetic influences than their fathers had been. In addition, they were working in a remote northern geographical area less culturally sophisticated than the Flemish cities, and among a population predominantly Calvinistic in its attitudes. All of these circumstances could be expected to tone down the flamboyance of the ceramic designs of the south.

By the first quarter of the seventeenth century, the Madonnas, the extravagant grotesques of Urbino, the spectacular peacock feather designs, and the highly formal alternating panels and fish scales of Deruta had given way, in Holland, to much simpler patterns. Of the original favorite Italian motifs, only the *aigrette*-and-*putto* (Figs. 9, 10), the vine, leaf, and flower (Fig. 15), and the massed pomegranates and grapes (Pl. 3) still retained their vigor in the decoration of Dutch majolica. Often found in the majolica patterns of the early seventeenth century are echoes from the archaic (thirteenth- and fourteenth-century) *maiolica* of Italy, in motifs such as the latticework, the stylized palm fronds, and certain border designs.

The use of plastic relief patterns and *impasto* (thickened color giving a light relief), frequent on Italian *maiolica* of the fourteenth and fifteenth centuries, seems not to have been employed by the Dutch potters except in a restrained version involving small, pushed-up roundels circling the edges of dishes, in the period around 1600.

Fig. 15. Dutch majolica dish, first half of the seventeenth century, in an Italianate vine-and-leaf motif combined with a geometric design, shown with a sherd from Fort Orange having the same center design.
(Dish) *Albany Institute of History and Art*
(Sherd and photo) *New York State Office of Parks, Recreation and Historic Preservation*

During the first half of the seventeenth century, except for the popularity of the single Chinese Ming pattern, the two dominant design influences on Dutch majolica were Italian and geometric. This changed in the second half of the century, when the majolica industry of Holland bowed to Delft, and eventually moved to Friesland, at which time the decoration shifted to a Dutch vernacular.

DISTINGUISHING FEATURES

Although Dutch majolica was the forerunner and prototype of Dutch fayence, it differs from the latter in the following particulars: (1) Although the front (obverse) side has a clear white glaze, the reverse side is covered by what is essentially a lead glaze, which, though it usually contains traces of tin oxide in its composition, appears always more drab and discolored than the white tin glaze of fayence; often, the glaze on the reverse side of Dutch majolica of the 1600-1660 period shows traces of a copperish green. (2) The obverse side of a majolica dish or plate displays three small, unglazed areas in the center, spaced in a triangular pattern, resulting from the *proenen* (supports) on which the piece rested during firing.[21] (3) The predominant decorative influence on Dutch majolica derives from Italian fayence with designs taken from classical/religious ther 〵, geometric figures, and fruits and flowers. (4) Only one Chinese design, the so-called Wan-li border, consisting of Chinese symbols and stylized chrysanthemums, with a center design of mandarin figures or of birds, rocks, and flowers, occurs on Dutch majolica. (5) The body is generally thicker than that of Dutch fayence, and the *grand feu* colors[22] more vivid. In early seventeenth-century examples of majolica, the body is often reddish in hue, though the later ware has a buff body similar to that of fayence.

REDISCOVERY OF MAJOLICA

Dutch people of discrimination have always valued the fayence of Delft for its charm and technical excellence, and the rest of the ceramics-conscious world was directed to it when Henry Havard published his *Histoire de la faïence de Delft* in 1878.[23] Yet Havard gave short shrift to the old Dutch majolica, dismissing it as *"faïence grossière"* and seeming to appreciate neither its important technical heritage nor its aesthetic qualities. Perhaps this is one reason for its being so long eclipsed by fayence.

According to Bernard Rackham, credit for reintroducing the early Dutch majolica to Dutch awareness in the twentieth century belongs to Dr. A. Pit, who in 1903 in the fourth annual *Bulletin* of the *Nederlandsche Oudheidkundige Bond* "first threw light on the obscurity which enshrouded the origin of the manufacture of enamelled [tin-glazed] earthenware in Holland."[24] This new awareness of the old earthenware was triggered by the finding of dated potsherds during the widening of a canal in Delft in 1902 and 1903. Six years later Dr. Pit followed up his earlier article with another, published in *Oud Holland*.[25]

In 1914, more majolica sherds were recovered when ground was being cleared for a new *Stadthuis* in Rotterdam. Then-director of the museum in Rotterdam, A. Hoynck van Papendrecht, pointed out the special significance of this discovery, inasmuch as it included kiln wasters and *proenen*.[26]

A landfill on Waalseiland in Amsterdam laid down in 1646 was excavated in the early years of this century when the Scheepvaarthuis was built, and this produced an interesting collection of sherds (Fig. 16). However, since the site had been occupied both before and after the landfill, and the excavation was made without controlled archaeological procedures, the sherds cannot be exactly dated.[27]

All of these discoveries led to a new interest in the old ware and to the publication of significant articles in several Dutch scholarly magazines. Elisabeth Neurdenburg, a Dutch scholar, wrote a book, *Old Dutch Pottery and Tiles*, in which she discussed majolica, though inadequately, and this was translated into English by Bernard Rackham, then the leading English authority on tin-glazed earthenwares.[28] Rackham himself soon published a book, *Early Netherlands Maiolica*, which is a fine historical study of early classic examples of the ware, but which stops short of discussing the more common majolica types of the first half of the seventeenth century that concern us in America.[29]

Nevertheless, unlike Havard, Rackham had a genuine appreciation for the qualities that give Dutch majolica its peculiar appeal. He admired its

Fig. 16. Blue-and-white and polychrome Dutch majolica sherds recovered in Amsterdam during excavation of the Nieuw Waalseiland site for construction of the Scheepvaarthuis. A landfill was made there in 1646, but these sherds cannot be positively dated to that time since no proper records of the excavation were kept.

However, all may be dated stylistically to the first half of the seventeenth century, and all have decorative elements found on sherds from Fort Orange.
Royal Dutch Antiquarian Society; on loan to the Rijksmuseum

similarities to Italian *maiolica,* and wrote enthusiastically of "the original style of decoration, with its charming freedom of design and attractive polychrome colouring [that] was early banished under pressure of the influence of imported Chinese blue and white porcelain, and scarcely survived after the middle of the 17th century." He went on to declare that "its loss was ill compensated for by the finer technique and carefully painted *chinoiseries* in blue [fayence] already in the ascendant as early as 1650."[30]

This was written in 1918, four years after the discovery of the majolica sherds on the *Stadthuis* site in Rotterdam that brought seventeenth-century Dutch majolica to the awareness of the post-World War I generation of ceramics students. Apparently, this interest did not penetrate to America at that time.

Neurdenburg's and Rackham's books are far from being adequate studies of important aspects of Dutch majolica that interest those of us in America now concerned with the specifics of archaeological artifacts, but they were extremely valuable at the time of their publication for creating an interest in this ware in English-speaking circles. Since that time, almost nothing about Dutch majolica has appeared in English-language publications.

Because Dutch majolica is so little understood in America, many archaeologists continue to classify it as delft, apparently preferring to ignore that though the two are closely related, they are separate ceramic entities, with different decorative emphases and spanning different time periods, and that these differences provide a valuable key for dating archaeological sites and specimens.

Lately, general interest in Dutch majolica (as distinct from fayence [delft]) has grown, and persons in the Netherlands and America are actively studying it through archaeological and documentary research.[31] No adequate book about it has yet been published in English, but Dingeman Korf's books of 1973 and 1981 offer much information to the English reader willing to familiarize himself with a few Dutch words and phrases.[32] J. D. van Dam's article detailing his studies has a splendid English summary,[33] as do articles appearing from time to time in *Oud Holland.* Of the latter, there is a useful review of the early studies of Dutch majolica and fayence in the English summary of Hessel Miedema's 1983 article on Northern Netherlandish majolica.[34]

It appears that in some quarters Dutch majolica is now receiving the recognition hitherto denied it, a matter of interest to Americans in several allied professional fields since that ware was used so widely in our seventeenth-century colonial settlements.

The exact way in which majolica and fayence were employed in New Netherland households can only be speculated upon, since no contemporary accounts of this seem to be available. It appears likely, however, that, as in the Netherlands at that time, these dishes functioned as status symbols and were used here more in a decorative capacity than as dining equipment. This is borne out by New Netherland household inventories and auction records, which list more pewter than earthenware dishes, indicating that the former were more generally used as tableware.

Early Dutch majolica dishes and plates, and those of fayence as well, had holes pierced in footrings at the time of manufacture to facilitate hanging them. That this was the custom among families of Dutch descent in New Netherland in the seventeenth and first half of the eighteenth centuries is supported by a passage from Dr. Alexander Hamilton's diary of his travels in America in the year 1744. He wrote of Albany: "[The Dutch here] set out their cabinets and buffets much with china, [and] they hang earthen or delft plates and dishes all around the walls, in manner of pictures, having a hole drilled thro' the edge of the plate or dish, and a loop or ribbon put into it to hang it by. . . ."[35] This is a prime example of the persistence of the original Dutch habits in material culture many years after the Dutch of New York were politically anglicized.

Fig. 17. Majolica "pancake" dish, first half of the seventeenth century. This name derives from the convex center of these dishes. The parrot design shown here, which does not appear in Korf's book on Dutch majolica, is a rare one and contains elements of the Wan-li design used uncharacteristically.
Private Owner

Notes - Chapter 13

1. David Whitehouse, "The Origins of Italian Maiolica," *Archaeology* 31 (1978): 49.
2. A design technique employing white on white.
3. Cipriano Piccolpasso, *The Three Books of the Potter's Art*, trans. Bernard Rackham and Albert van der Put (London: Victoria and Albert Museum, 1934).
4. A narrative style of ceramic decoration in classical, biblical or historical themes, in which the design covers the entire surface of the dish, leaving no border.
5. The Italo-Flemish potters who went to England set up potteries that produced a majolica often difficult to distinguish from Dutch majolica. For a discussion of this English ware, see Ivor Noël Hume, *Early English Delftware from London and Virginia*, Colonial Williamsburg Occasional Papers in Archaeology, no. 2 (Williamsburg: Colonial Williamsburg Foundation, 1977).
6. Jan Baart, "Ceramiche italiane rinvenute in Olanda e le prime imitazioni olandesi" (trans. Melinda Yates), in *Atti, XVI Convegno Internazionale della Ceramica* (Albisola, Italy: Centro Ligure per la Storia della Ceramica, 1983), 162.
7. Ibid., 169.
8. Ibid.
9. Ferrand Hudig, "Wapengoet en porceleyn," *Oud Holland* 43 (1926): 165.
10. As far as this author knows, there is no majolica now being made in the Netherlands, although there are potteries in Friesland and at Delft making attractive fayence.
11. Hudig, "Wapengoet en porceleyn," 162-81.
12. The makers of this new type of tin-glazed earthenware (fayence), like some modern manufacturers, made misleading claims for their product, often advertising it as "porceleyn" and themselves as porcelain makers.
13. Information about the sources from which the Dutch obtained their clays in the seventeenth century was furnished me in a letter by J. D. van Dam, curator of the Princessehof Museum, Leeuwarden. Mr. van Dam's research in Dutch archives has corrected earlier misconceptions about this.
14. See chapter 1, note 16.
15. Brigitte Tietzel, *Fayence* (Cologne: Kunstgewerbemuseum der Stadt, 1980), 28.
16. The sediment from wine casks that has been burned.
17. A partly fused mass.
18. Formulae for the majolica glaze vary considerably among writers on the subject. The one given here is based on information from three sources: *Encyclopaedia Britannica,* 11th ed., 5:737; Anthony Ray, *English Delftware Pottery* (Boston: Boston Book and Art Shop, 1968), 86; and Alan Caiger-Smith,

Tin-Glaze Pottery (London: Faber and Faber, 1973), Appendix B.

19. Clay boxes that protect ceramic objects while they are in the kiln.

20. Dingeman Korf, *Nederlandse majolica*, 4th ed. (Bussum: 1973), 43-44.

21. A Dutch friend with experience with majolica told the author that he has occasionally seen pieces of majolica with saggar support marks underneath the rim on the reverse side instead of *proen* scars on the obverse.

22. Pigments that can endure a temperature high enough to fire the glaze.

23. Henry Havard, *Histoire de la faïence de Delft,* 2 vols. (Paris: E. Plon et Cie., 1878).

24. Bernard Rackham, "Early Dutch Maiolica and Its English Kindred," *Burlington Magazine* 33 (1918): 116. This article contains much general material about Dutch majolica, as well as its relationship to English-made majolica of the first half of the seventeenth century. Unfortunately, in his conclusion, Rackham allows himself to be diverted by the now-discounted contribution of the Dutch artist Hendrik Vroom to the development of Dutch majolica.

25. A. Pit, "Oude Noord-Nederlandsche majolica," *Oud Holland* 27 (1909): 133-41.

26. Rackham, "Early Dutch Maiolica," 116.

27. Hessel Miedema, "Noordnederlandse majolica: kast opruimen," *Oud Holland* 97 (1983): 231.

28. Elisabeth Neurdenburg, *Old Dutch Pottery and Tiles*, ed. and trans. Bernard Rackham (New York: Himebaugh and Browne, 1923).

29. Rackham, *Early Netherlands Maiolica* (London: Geoffrey Bles, 1926).

30. Rackham, "Early Dutch Maiolica," 123.

31. With the building of the subway in Amsterdam and the clearing of large areas in the older parts of that city for urban renewal, archaeologists there are finding quantities of early Dutch majolica. Likewise, work on the polders in the North Sea region is revealing majolica from sunken ships that had lain concealed under water for several centuries.

32. Korf, *Nederlandse majolica*, 4th ed. (Bussum: 1973); ibid., 5th ed. (Haarlem: De Haan, 1981).

33. J. D. van Dam, "Geleyersgoet en Hollants porceleyn: Ontwikkelingen in de Nederlandse aardewerk-industrie, 1560-1660," *Mededelingenblad, Nederlandse vereniging van vrienden van de ceramiek* 108 (1982/84): 88-92.

34. Miedema, "Noordnederlandse majolica," 253-56.

35. Alexander Hamilton, *Itinerarium* (St. Louis: Bixby, 1907) 87-88.

14
Dutch Fayence

Seventeenth-century Dutch fayence[1] is a technical extension of Dutch majolica, since it is made of the same basic materials and in much the same way as the latter. Yet it cannot be considered the same product as majolica because of differences in period, design emphasis, form, and methods of manufacture (Pls. 6, 12; Figs. 8, 18, 19, 30, 31).

In its transferral from Spain to Italy, tin-glazed earthenware forsook most of its Middle Eastern design elements to take on certain Italian motifs that reflected Gothic or Renaissance influences. These designs, in turn, were transferred to Dutch majolica, to which Dutch potters then added North Netherlandish traditional design motifs.

Dutch fayence, on the other hand, from the first derived its primary decorative inspiration from Chinese porcelain, with only now and then a backward gesture toward the Italian motifs so pervasive in Dutch majolica. It is therefore impossible to discuss Dutch fayence without touching upon the introduction of Chinese porcelain into Europe, probably first by Venetian traders, later by the Portuguese and the Spanish, in the sixteenth century. Most Europeans remained ignorant of the charms of Chinese porcelain until the early years of the seventeenth century, however.

In 1602 the Dutch, then at war with Portugal, captured the *San Jago*, a carrack on its way home from China with porcelain and other luxuries.[2] The cargo was sold at public auction at Middelburg at great profit, and this event seems to have been the beginning of a love affair between the Dutch and the Oriental porcelain that was to have vast influence on Dutch ceramic history, and even on the course of all European ceramics for two centuries to come.

The introduction of Chinese porcelain into Italy had inspired there an attempt to copy it in its own medium. Francesco de' Medici, Grand Duke of Tuscany, is usually credited with inaugurating this project around the year 1575.[3] The result was a soft-paste porcelain with glass frit as its decisive ingredient, and a decoration in blue and white based primarily on Chinese designs. This Medici porcelain is marked in underglaze blue with a drawing of the dome of the cathedral at Florence, below which is the letter "F" in script. The manufacture of this artificial porcelain continued for only about twenty years, and the relatively few examples that have survived bring large sums on the antiques market.

The Dutch, unlike the Florentines, had no wealthy patron interested in underwriting so expensive a process as experimental porcelain manufacture, and apparently their good sense told them that the most profitable way to exploit the Oriental porcelain was by a two-pronged approach: to import it from China and sell it to those who could afford it, and, for the large majority who could not, to manufacture the best possible copy, using the old majolica techniques already at hand.

According to van Dam, regular imports of Chinese porcelain into Holland were begun around 1620,[4] which seems a rather tardy start when it is considered that the Dutch East India Company had been operating profitably since 1602. The exact time at which the manufacture of fayence commenced in Holland is not recorded, but van Dam in the article previously cited gives the important transition years from majolica to fayence as 1620 to 1635. By the 1640s the manufacture of fayence was becoming common, and by 1660 it had displaced majolica in most areas of the Netherlands.

During the transitional period when both fayence and majolica were being produced in Holland, individual pieces often showed atypical characteristics. Sometimes, proto-fayence plates have a crudeness of fabrication and design more characteristic of the earlier majolica. Several pieces of this type were recovered at the site of Fort Orange (Albany, New York) (Pl. 5). Conversely, the later majolica often has qualities usually associated with fayence. The author owns a large sherd of an eight-inch majolica dish whose smoothness and brilliance of glaze and Chinese flower-in-vase design make it appear to be fayence, until the *proen* marks on the obverse and the lead-glazed reverse are noted.

The word *delft* was attached to Dutch fayence many years after the industry became centered in the city of Delft. It should be understood, however, that the earliest pieces of this improved ware were probably made in Haarlem or Amsterdam, and that it almost certainly continued to be made in those places into the second half of the seventeenth century, and perhaps later.[5]

Fig. 18. Dutch fayence cups (ca. 1665-1680) excavated in 1982 at the Waterlooplein site, Amsterdam, Holland.
Amsterdam Historical Museum; photos *DOW/AHM Department of Archaeology, Amsterdam, Holland*

MANUFACTURING TECHNIQUES

Production practices for Dutch fayence diverged from the majolica techniques in several particulars. Its delicacy of form and need for quality control demanded that it be protected from the flames and smoke of the kiln, so dishes were now fired suspended on supports inserted within saggars instead of being stacked on *proenen* in the open kiln, as majolica was (Fig. 8). In addition, the clay body of fayence was more carefully refined for the removal of impurities, and pieces were designed in more sophisticated shapes and reduced to a thinness equal to that of some examples of Chinese porcelain.

DECORATION

This new earthenware employed the entire range of Chinese blue-and-white decorative themes contemporary with its beginnings, whereas majolica's Sino-decorative emphasis had been largely limited to variants of one particular late Ming design known today as the Wan-li pattern. This is distinguished by a wide, paneled border of stylized Chinese symbols and flowers in medallions, and by a center design of birds, rocks, and flowers (commonly known now as the bird-on-a-rock pattern) (Fig. 29). Sometimes the center design is a Chinese mandarin figure on a terrace (Fig. 12). Variants of this design in fayence were popular in the Netherlands well into the eighteenth century.

Although Chinese motifs dominated the decorative designs of Dutch fayence during its heyday, Italian and native Dutch themes were also popular. In the seventeenth century, however, these latter two rarely found their way to America as export types.

In ceramic studies an understanding of colors and color processes, as well as of decorative sources, is of great practical use, since these have vast significance in dating specimens—a consideration of major importance to curators, archaeologists, and collectors. Early Dutch fayence was decorated only in cobalt blue, like the Chinese porcelain the Dutch potters were copying (Fig. 19). After a time, however, manganese and other colors were employed. This first use of polychrome on Dutch fayence (as previously on majolica) involved what are known as *grand feu* colors, that is, colors derived from pigments that can withstand kiln temperatures high enough to fire the glaze of earthenwares.

Toward the end of the seventeenth century, two new colors were introduced on a limited scale by at least two of the factories at Delft—a red made from an ochreous clay called Armenian bole,[6] and gold.[7] This kind of decoration was very expensive, in both materials and labor costs, and was used on only

Fig. 19. Blue-and-white Dutch fayence chocolate cups recovered from two Seneca Indian village sites in western New York, dating from the third quarter of the seventeenth century.
Rochester Museum and Science Center, Rochester, New York

luxury types of fayence. Consequently, it was not likely to have been imported into America at that period, and so is not of great concern to American archaeologists. It is, however, of concern to American museum curators and collectors.

Unlike Dutch majolica, the fayence was often given an extra coating of lead glaze to increase its durability and brilliance, and to make it more like the Chinese porcelain in appearance. This second application of glaze is called *kwaart* by the Dutch.

MODERN BOOKS ON DUTCH FAYENCE

There has been no book on Dutch fayence published in English that entirely fulfills the needs of American curators, archaeologists, and collectors. *Delft Ceramics* by C. H. de Jonge places the empha-

sis strongly on the locations of the individual potteries in Delft, their chronology, and their owners and directors at various periods. Important though these matters may be to the history of ceramics, it is the product itself that most concerns Americans, and de Jonge's book leaves fundamental questions relating to it unanswered. The book is copiously illustrated, and the author, in her foreword, claims that it "so far as possible treats of the less familiar pieces." Certainly the illustrations are well chosen and suitable for the kind of book it is—a formal basic work on Delft potters and pottery. But for the most part, the fayence shown is of a high quality rarely to be found outside the Netherlands.[8]

A more recent work, available in English, is *Delftware: Faience Production at Delft,* by Henry-Pierre Fourest, curator-in-chief of the Musée National de Céramique, at Sèvres. This is a handsome quarto volume filled with magnificent illustrations, many of which are in color. Fourest restricts his main explanatory text to 36 out of the 201 pages that make up the book but fully compensates for this with comprehensive, descriptive paragraphs appended to the 180 illustrative plates. These illustrations, particularly those in color, are of magnificent quality, many with such clear detail that one has the sensation of examining actual pieces of fayence. The author's forte lies in analyzing designs and their historical origins, but he is less lucid when discussing technical matters. He uses the term "faience" loosely, both to describe dishes with *proen* marks on the obverse that are obviously majolica, and also in speaking of the pottery of Delft.[9] Now and then Fourest voices opinions strange to this writer, such as his theory about the small holes on the undersides of fayence dishes.[10] Moreover, the Dutch name inscribed on an impressive dish pictured in the work is carelessly transcribed.[11] Yet Fourest's book is outstanding for the quality of its illustrations, which alone contribute much to its usefulness for the student of Dutch fayence.

There is, however, drastic need for books on this subject that are of a more down-to-earth quality, with text and illustrations that concern dishes made for use by middle-income families or for export to colonies settled by persons of limited means, as were the Dutch colonies in North America. Unfortunately, no such book is today available in English, and the writing of one demands a knowledge of the subject that few but the Dutch possess—to say nothing of access to original examples of this non-museum kind of ware.

Now and then catalogs published in connection with special museum exhibits introduce a refreshing note into the majolica/fayence discussion, in the form of dishes with less hackneyed designs and of a less elitist nature than those portrayed in the standard works. The article "Geleyersgoet en Hollants porceleyn: Ontwikkelingen in de Nederlandse aardewerk-industrie, 1560-1660" by J. D. van Dam concerns a fine exhibit of these two types of earthenware assembled jointly in 1982 by the Princessehof Museum of Leeuwarden (Friesland) and the Frans Hals Museum of Haarlem. This catalog, in Dutch but with an English summary, has fine illustrations showing the type of middle-quality fayence so rarely found in books, and thus so helpful to the student. The catalog is strong in Frisian ceramics, which were not produced for export in Makkum and Harlingen until toward the end of the New Netherland period, and consequently are not likely to show up on American sites of the New Netherland period in any numbers.

Another source of information about Dutch tin-glazed wares is the magazine *Oud Holland*, which now and then publishes important articles on these wares, lately accompanied by English summaries. The earlier issues of the magazine carried material on this subject that is now of great importance in chronicling the entire history of tin-glazed earthenware in the Netherlands. Unfortunately, these do not have summaries in English.

DUTCH TILES

The earliest tiles made in northern Europe after the departure of the Romans were plain floor tiles in red earthenware with a lead glaze. From these there evolved a more sophisticated floor tile, in which elaborate designs were incised into the clay body, and these then filled with a light slip over which a lead glaze was applied. Many of these tiles were extremely fine aesthetically, even though they were restricted to the colors brown, buff, and sometimes green. But this kind of tile was expensive for those times (the Middle Ages and later), and their use was generally confined to churches and wealthy religious houses.

Ornamental tin-glazed tiles for floors had been introduced into the Spanish Netherlands (at Antwerp) about the same time as were majolica dishes but were found to be impractical because the decoration was too quickly worn away. Very soon, however, such tiles were transferred to the interior walls of houses, where they not only created a pleasing and colorful background for furnishings, but were also easy to clean—two qualities valued by the Dutch *huysvrouw*. The earliest of these were in polychrome and had a red body deriving from local sedimentary sea and river clays—"fat" clays in which iron was plentiful. In the seventeenth century, the importa-tion of clays high in chalk content from Belgium and England resulted in a buff-colored body for fayence tiles.

The earliest wall tiles were reported to be as much as one inch thick, but by the second quarter of the seventeenth century, tiles of not more than three-eighths of an inch (11 mm) thick were common, and this was reduced still further in subsequent times, such that later tiles were often made no more than one-quarter of an inch in thickness. These progressive changes in the color and thickness of tiles have resulted in a general rule for dating them: the redder and thicker the body, the older the tile.

Polychrome flowers and fruits with stylized foliations usually in dark blue formed the decoration for the earliest of the Dutch tin-glazed wall tiles. An early favorite motif was the pomegranate, soon followed by grapes and tulips. Green, orange, and a dark cobalt blue were the prevailing colors. Animals, birds, and human figures all appeared before 1600 in the decoration of Dutch tiles—a decoration heavily concentrated, with very little white background left exposed. The human figures on these early tiles were large, covering much of the width of the tile, but by the middle of the seventeenth century, figures had become smaller.

For a time, Dutch polychrome tiles had no individual corner designs as distinct from the overall design, but by the end of the first quarter of the seventeenth century, specific corner designs were popular for tiles. Among the earliest of these were the *fleur de lis* (stylized into a spearhead appearance) and a late Ming-inspired fret. The ox-head motif and, later, the so-called spider-head were other popular corner designs for fayence tiles of the seventeenth century. These are important not particularly for their decorative value, which in the case of the latter two was negligible, but for their usefulness in dating tiles.[12]

It is obviously impossible to describe here all pictorial motifs used on Dutch tiles in the seventeenth century since they covered the wide range of Dutch interests and activities of that day. There are, however, certain distinctive patterns that are useful in helping us identify tiles by their time period. Three motifs that can be used in this way are the shaped roundel (sometimes scalloped), the shaped medallion, and the plain circle, all of which are used as frames for a central figure. Both the shaped roundel and the shaped Chinese Ming-style medallion belong to the first quarter of the seventeenth century. The plain circle came slightly later and attained its greatest popularity in the first half of the eighteenth century.

A distinctive and thoroughly Dutch form useful as a dating tool for tiles is the tulip, which was used before 1600 on polychrome tiles in a stylized form, and in the 1630s and 1640s, on both tiles and dishes, more naturalistically as a single plant standing upright in the ground, though sometimes with head drooping, or in a formal flower arrangement in a vase. These later tulip tiles are often in polychrome, sometimes in blue and white, but, unlike its earlier use in a crowded design, the flower now stands in an expanse of white. The popularity of this design continued throughout the third quarter of the seventeenth century.

Other specific milestones in the chronology of Dutch decorative tiles are soldier tiles, first appearing around 1600, but particularly associated with the second quarter of the seventeenth century; compote-and-fruit tiles of the same period; tiles with small, isolated animal or human figures surrounded by a large expanse of white, third quarter of the seventeenth century;[13] and blue and white tiles showing pastoral and biblical scenes (usually encircled)[14] and children's games, dating from the fourth quarter of the seventeenth century.

Picture tiles made of standard five-inch wall tiles but used in elaborate murals large enough to cover an entire section of a room and smaller quadrate designs made for framing were an important aspect of Dutch seventeenth-century tile manufacture. They have little relevance for this book, however, since at least the former were too expensive and sophisticated in conception to have been a part of New Netherland furnishings.

For some years the standard works on Dutch tiles published in English were those of Dingeman Korf and C. H. de Jonge.[15] Both of these have helpful chapters on manufacturing techniques, in addition to lengthy discussions of designs. In 1984, the Philadelphia Museum of Art, with support from other organizations, published a catalog of its own superb collection of Dutch tiles.[16] This work of impeccable scholarship was written and edited by a group of Dutch and American experts in the field and is the best study of Dutch tiles yet produced in America, perhaps anywhere. The illustrations are particularly fine.

Notes - Chapter 14

1. The word *fayence* is used in this book to designate the earthenware habitually referred to in America as "delft."
2. J. D. van Dam, "Geleyersgoet en Hollants porceleyn: Ontwikkelingen in de Nederlandse aardewerk-industrie, 1560-1660," *Mededelingenblad, Nederlandse vereniging van vrienden van de ceramiek* 108 (1982/84): 13.
3. At this period Europeans did not know that in order to make true porcelain it was necessary to combine a clay rich in naturally decomposed feldspar (kaolin) with pulverized feldspar (China stone, called *petunse* by the Chinese).
4. Van Dam, "Geleyersgoet en Hollants porceleyn," 88.
5. See Verstraeten case in chapter 13.
6. Since the fifteenth century, the Turkish (Isnik) and Italian potters had used Armenian bole successfully. The Chinese, whose porcelain the Dutch were copying in fayence, very early employed a red made from copper oxide, which proved difficult to control because of its unpredictability under kiln temperatures. By the fifteenth century they were using a red made from iron oxide, a more stable compound, and presumably this was used later by Dutch potters.
7. Caroline H. de Jonge, *Delft Ceramics* (New York: Praeger, 1970), 71.
8. A more satisfactory book by the same author is *Oud-Nederlandsche majolica en Delftsch aardewerk, 1550-1800* (Amsterdam: Scheltema en Holkema, 1947), but this has not been translated into English.
9. Henry-Pierre Fourest, *Delftware: Faience Production at Delft*, trans. Katherine Watson (New York: Rizzoli, 1980), plates 3-5.
10. Ibid., 17.
11. Ibid., 81.
12. For an excellent summary of corner motifs on Dutch tiles, see Philadelphia Museum of Art, *Dutch Tiles in the Philadelphia Museum of Art* (New Haven: Eastern Press, 1984), 174-77.
13. Very large human and animal figures in polychrome denote a date of around 1600. Because of their early date, these are unlikely ever to have been used in the American settlements.
14. Encircled biblical scenes in manganese, often with chapter and verse citations, belong to the first half of the eighteenth century. Many houses in the Hudson Valley and elsewhere in eastern New York built in the second quarter of the eighteenth century had these.
15. Dingeman Korf, *Dutch Tiles* (New York: Universe Books, 1964); De Jonge, *Dutch Tiles*, trans. P. S. Falla (New York: Praeger, 1971).
16. Philadelphia Museum of Art, *Dutch Tiles in the Philadelphia Museum of Art*.

15

Foreign Wares Distributed by the Dutch

One of the factors that enabled the early Dutch to become the successful traders they were was their appreciation of the value of miscellany as an element in trade. Even when the particular purpose of a Dutch trading expedition was to buy or sell bulk commodities such as grain, timber, furs or tobacco, the ships' manifests usually included a record of small consumer goods for exchange when the opportunity arose. In this manner, not only Dutch manufactures but the goods of other nations as well were distributed in many obscure regions by the Dutch.

GERMAN STONEWARE

High on the list of foreign goods carried in Dutch trading vessels in the early seventeenth century was German salt-glazed stoneware from the Rhine provinces. This was basically of two types: a gray-and-blue stoneware from the Westerwald consisting mainly of drinking vessels, and brown-mottled stoneware jugs from Frechen, near Cologne. Examples of these two types (both called *Krüge* in German), in the form of sherds, are found in great numbers on American seventeenth-century sites where the Dutch settled or traded.

Although there are archaeologists in America who appear to believe that all Rhenish stoneware found on the sites of early English settlements in this country arrived there by transhipment from England, this is patently not true. The Dutch are known to have supplied England with this ware in the sixteenth and seventeenth centuries, and in view of their documented commerce with America in the first half of the seventeenth century, the weight of evidence is that they also brought the Rhenish stonewares here during that period. One must agree with Thwaite, who concluded that "most Rhenish stoneware was carried to England and elsewhere in Netherlandish ships."[1]

WESTERWALD STONEWARE

The Westerwald, a district of the ancient Duchy of Nassau in Germany, is a heavily forested and moun-

tainous area lying east of the Rhine River and just south of Westphalia. In the seventeenth century, following the decline of the potting industry in Siegburg (Westphalia) as a result of the Thirty Years' War, the Westerwald became an important stoneware center because of its fine clay deposits and abundance of wood, the latter being necessary to support the high firing temperatures required for the manufacture of stoneware.

We have come to associate Westerwald stoneware with the blue-and-gray color combination though it was also made in other colors in that region, as, for example, the light-colored latticework pieces in the manner of Siegburg. In the late sixteenth and early seventeenth centuries, some of the blue-and-gray drinking forms made in the Westerwald were elaborate in shape and decoration. The ones brought to America by the Dutch had some of the varied and intricate designs typical of this ware but were relatively simple in shape (Pl. 11; Figs. 20, 21).

Fig. 20. Blue-on-gray Rhenish stoneware *Krug* with arms of Amsterdam. This is from Gannagaro (1670-1687), a Seneca-Iroquois site in western New York State.
Rochester Museum and Science Center

Fig. 21. Seventeenth-century Westerwald stoneware *Krug* from a
Seneca-Iroquois site (1660-1675) in western New York.
Rochester Museum and Science Center

A particularly handsome stoneware, café-au-lait in color and with a diagonal latticework design, was made toward the end of the sixteenth century and at the beginning of the seventeenth at Siegburg and Raeren. The Germans appear to have several descriptive names for this type of stoneware, among them *Netzornament, Netzwerk,* and *Kerbschnitt* (Fig. 22). This distinctive latticework pattern most frequently occurs on the shoulders and lower half of a drinking vessel, usually with an ornamental frieze separating the two parts. The pattern is so deeply incised as to appear to have been carved in the paste while it was in the leather state, and the use of the term *Kerbschnitt* (notch-cut) supports this idea. It has been suggested that sherds of this type found in America may have been made at Höhr in the Westerwald, which carried on the Siegburg potting tradition.

Fig. 22. German stoneware *Krug* with a type of decoration known as *Netzornament,* early seventeenth century. The prototype of this jug was manufactured at Seigburg in the sixteenth century. Sherds of similar pieces were found at Fort Orange and the Stadt-huys site in New York City.
Sleepy Hollow Restorations, Tarrytown, New York

The body of most Westerwald stoneware is gray. The unglazed inner surface of the hollow wares is sometimes gray and sometimes a dull, rose pink, of a shade once called *bois-de-rose.* This rather attractive variation in color may reflect the amount of oxygen that reached the inner surface of the piece during firing. Occasionally, one sees what appear to be Westerwald sherds that have a cream- or buff-colored body and inner surface. These may be of Flemish origin.

As the seventeenth century advanced, incised decoration began to replace to a noticeable extent the earlier raised type of decoration on Westerwald stoneware. A rather large and boldly delineated flower motif came into favor toward the end of the century and continued to be prominent in the decoration of Westerwald mugs throughout the eighteenth century.

Because the decorative motifs on Westerwald *Krüge* changed appreciably over the years and such changes are well documented in books, sherds of this ware constitute good dating tools for archaeological sites. In the late nineteenth century and early twentieth, prior to World War I, German potteries were turning out thousands of replicas of the early Westerwald drinking vessels for the American market. Many of these are easily recognizable as reproductions, but some are not. Since there are few examples of this ware on exhibit in American museums today, the average American student of ceramics has little opportunity to become familiar with its characteristics. A good book in English on those German wares would be of great assistance to archaeologists and collectors.

COLOGNE AND FRECHEN STONEWARE JUGS

The brown-mottled stoneware jugs made at Frechen, a suburb of Cologne (Köln), in Germany, are found widely on American archaeological sites in the areas of seventeenth-century Dutch trade (Pls. 9, 10). These are correctly known as *Bartmannkrüge,* from the mask of a bearded man that adorns the neck of the jug, just below the lip. English antiquarians and archaeologists have long called these "Bellarmine" jugs, from an incident involving an unpopular cardinal of that name of whom the unpleasant mask was said to be reminiscent. Today, the German name is preferred by most of those working in the field of historical ceramics.

In the sixteenth century, the finest specimens of this ceramic type were made in Cologne, a city of unusually talented potters. The Cologne jugs had a skillfully modelled mask, naturalistic and rather benevolent in expression, and a neatly delineated beard. The body of the jug, below the mask, was globular in shape, and was usually decorated with elaborate designs, or with medallions containing complex armorial devices of municipalities or prominent nobles and churchmen (Fig. 23). Several sherds of Cologne-type Bartmann jugs were recovered on the site of Fort Orange.

Fig. 23. Rhenish stoneware jug, mid-seventeenth century. The arms of the city of Cologne decorate this fragment of a Bartmann jug from Schuyler Flatts.
New York State Office of Parks, Recreation and Historic Preservation

Late in the sixteenth century, much of the stoneware industry in Cologne shifted to nearby Frechen, although the former city continued to be its distribution point. The shift was accompanied by a decline in workmanship and quality control. The bearded face became elongated and its modelling less naturalistic, which resulted in a somewhat disagreeable, if not threatening, expression. The oval medallions were less meticulously designed and molded than on the earlier Cologne ware, and the body of the jug became pear-shaped instead of globular, as formerly.

Often the medallion areas of the Bartmann jugs have dashes of cobalt blue over the brown. According to Thwaite, of twenty-nine Bartmann jugs examined in England bearing dates between 1594 and 1607, many showed such traces of blue.[2] This treatment appears to have declined as the seventeenth century advanced and may have been discontinued entirely by its second half.

The brown glaze on the Bartmann jugs varies from piece to piece. Some that belong to the first half of the seventeenth century have what are sometimes referred to as the "coagulated," starkly contrasted dark brown spots of the so-called tigerware (Fig. 24), while in others the brown is lighter and more evenly distributed, though patches of gray often intrude on the brown. As with Westerwald drinking vessels, the salt glaze produces a coarsely pitted appearance. The body color of the Frechen *Bartmannkrug* is a

medium gray, as is its unglazed inner surface. As the seventeenth century advanced, these jugs became progressively cruder in appearance and less attractive as ceramic forms.

Fig. 24. Frechen-type tigerware *Bartmannkrug* with the arms of Amsterdam, first half of the seventeenth century. Sherds of such pieces were found at Fort Orange, Schuyler Flatts, and the Van Buren site.
Museum of International Folk Art of the Museum of New Mexico, Sante Fe, New Mexico

In the Dutch East India trade, *Bartmannkrüge* were often used as containers for the quicksilver obtained from the Orient. In the western trade, they were primarily used in shipping spirits of various kinds, though also for molasses, vinegar, cider, and other common household liquids.

GERMAN UTILITY EARTHENWARES

From the thirteenth century, communities in western Germany along the Rhine River and its tributaries had been making lead-glazed earthenwares that combined utility with a high degree of aesthetic charm. Growing out of this industry, three wares emerged to be widely distributed by the Dutch wherever they traded in the sixteenth and seventeenth centuries. The names commonly given to these by archaeologists today are Weser, Werra, and Wanfried wares.

Weser ware, which takes its name from the Weser River valley area of its provenance, has a light yellow body sometimes merging into pink, and its decoration falls into two general styles that differ from each other in overall appearance. The first of these consists of a yellow ground, sometimes covered with rouletted lines, onto which surface are applied slip decorations in green and brown. These are characteristically rectilinear vertical designs or dots, or combinations of these motifs, over which the glaze is applied.[3] Another type of decoration characteristic of the lead-glazed Weser ware employs a white slip in a reddish-brown-and-yellow color combination with touches of green. Here motifs are somewhat more naturalistic, in that they often consist of birds or stylized flowers handled with a peasant-art technique, though applied slip decorations in linear forms are also common.[4] Weser ware in both these decorative types has been found archaeologically in Amsterdam in positions indicating that it was introduced into that city no earlier than around 1570 and ceased to be imported there around 1620.[5]

Werra ware is a red-bodied, slip-decorated earthenware that employs green in its design. Wanfried ware, also red-bodied and slip-decorated, is distinctive in its extravagant *sgraffito* work. This ware is commonly considered the inspiration for the Pennsylvania Dutch wares of the eighteenth and nineteenth centuries.

Although here we have characterized the German redwares as utility wares simply because those occurring on New York Dutch sites all seem to fall into that category, it must be pointed out that in many cases German redwares were decorated with high standards of artistry and sophistication. In the fifteenth and sixteenth centuries, Germany was a leader in European pottery skills and techniques, and produced superior wares of many kinds. The greatest of these were the stonewares, yet great care often went into the production of fine redware dishes, among these the Wanfried *sgraffito* wares with complicated incised designs. Large dishes of this kind, made primarily for decorative or formal purposes and not intended to be utilitarian, may be found in the Rijksmuseum and other leading museums of Europe.[6]

ITALIAN SLIPWARE

A red-bodied earthenware with a reddish, marbleized slip decoration, usually referred to by archaeologists as "North Italian slipware," turns up with some regularity on seventeenth-century American Atlantic seaboard sites where there has been Dutch settlement or trade. This has also been found archaeologically in England and the Netherlands (Fig. 25). Those examples found here are usually assumed to have been of either Dutch or English export, but, for the record, there is at least one seventeenth-century documentary reference implying that Venetian ships sometimes traded in Virginia and New England.[7]

Fig. 25. Italian redware bowl and matching sherds, seventeenth century. Found archaeologically in Holland, this northern Italian slipware bowl and the sherds from Fort Orange are a type of foreign ware imported into the Netherlands in the early seventeenth century and distributed widely by Dutch traders.
(Bowl) *Crailo State Historic Site, Rensselaer, New York*
(Sherds) *New York State Office of Parks, Recreation and Historic Preservation*

As an interesting example of ceramic design continuity that transcends limitations of time and geography, it may be noted that during the T'ang dynasty (618-906) a type of marbleized earthenware similar in appearance to this Italian ware was made in China and exported to Japan.[8] This was not, however, a slipware but was made in much the same way as the English eighteenth-century agate wares, by mixing different-colored clays.

ITALIAN FAYENCE

Several sherds of what appears to have been a lobed dish or vessel with a light, turquoise blue tin glaze were recovered from an important Hudson

Fig. 26. Detail from **Still Life with Turkey Pie**, by Pieter Claesz (1597-1660), showing a Chinese porcelain dish in the Wan-li pattern that was copied so widely by Dutch potters in majolica and fayence.
Rijksmuseum

River site (Schuyler Flatts, near Albany, New York) settled by the Dutch by 1643. A similar type was noted on an early Virginia plantation and on Massachusetts sites. This is believed to be a type of Italian fayence.

CHINESE PORCELAIN

From the time of the establishment of the Dutch East India Company in 1602, the Dutch were increasingly large importers of Chinese porcelain (Fig. 26). Within recent years, progress in underwater archaeology has made possible the salvage of several seventeenth-century Dutch ships with cargoes rich in this ware. Two of these ships, the *Witte Leeuw*, which sank in 1613, and the Hatcher-recovered ship (name unknown), which went down in 1643, carried impressive cargoes of porcelain that give a fine picture of the quality and designs then arriving in Holland.[9] However, as far as can be judged by the number of porcelain sherds recovered from early seventeenth-century American sites, little of this found its way across the Atlantic at that time. Undoubtedly, the reason for this was an economic one. Porcelain was expensive in comparison with the European ceramics available, and settlers attempting to establish themselves in America in the early seventeenth century were people of limited means, except for a very few privileged families. Sherds of Ming and Transition Period[10] porcelain brought here by the Dutch have been recovered, but these are few in number. In the second half of the century, however, more porcelain was imported, and by the early years of the eighteenth century, fine Chinese wares were reaching the North American continent in great quantity.

A QUESTION OF PROVENANCE

The incidence of Dutch ceramic material encountered today on English colonial sites in America has presented our archaeologists with a dilemma that has long dogged the profession in England: the difficulty of distinguishing between certain Dutch-made and English-made pieces. In the course of a large export trade that the Netherlands conducted with England in the sixteenth and early seventeenth centuries, Dutch majolica dishes were imported into

London in appreciable quantities. Since in the same general period majolica was being made in both Holland and England by Italo-Flemish potters using similar designs and techniques of manufacture, the Dutch wares and the English wares are often difficult to distinguish from each other.

A member of the ceramics department of a famous London museum showed this author a majolica plate excavated in London that for many years had been exhibited by the museum as of seventeenth-century English manufacture but is now believed to be

Fig. 27. *a.* Early seventeenth-century majolica dish of a type often difficult to attribute—to England or to Holland.
b. Reverse of dish showing pierced hole in footring for hanging typical of Dutch majolica.
Victoria and Albert Museum, London, England

Dutch. Some who have given much study to this matter believe that there are many pieces of Dutch majolica in British museums still incorrectly attributed (Fig. 27).

A further difficulty and cause of confusion is that Dutch potters of this early period preferred English clays and imported them whenever international conditions made this possible. Thus, English and Dutch majolica made in the first half of the seventeenth century (prior to the Anglo-Dutch wars) show no differences in the chemistry of body fabric.

There are some who believe that concern for establishing whether a piece of majolica is of English or Dutch manufacture has gone on too long and has become nonproductive—an opinion certainly deserving consideration. Yet those involved in the dichotomy of Dutch-English archaeological sites in America may find this attitude uncongenial. Accurate attribution of sherds has a legitimate bearing on chronology, trade patterns, material cultures, and other aspects of archaeology and history, and thus seems too pertinent to abandon without a struggle. American archaeologists have been at a disadvantage in regard to Dutch ceramics because American museum collections have been deficient in Dutch wares other than fayence (delft), and a similar imbalance exists among books about Dutch ceramics that have been available to them.

It is possible that in many instances keen observation and attention to small details could produce helpful clues in determining differences between the majolica made in England and that made in the Netherlands in the early seventeenth century. For example, in the collection of seventeenth-century ceramics at Jamestown, where, without question, there is some of each type, it was noticed that certain of the majolica sherds decorated in the familiar Wan-li pattern show a distinctive orange-shellac effect on the reverse side. The same thing was observed on some sherds in the laboratory of the London Museum. Conversely, none of the Wan-li-patterned sherds from Fort Orange or other upper Hudson River Dutch sites had this characteristic, nor did any observed at the municipal laboratory in Amsterdam. This proves nothing, but suggests a possible criterion.

Another characteristic to be noticed about much English-made majolica of the seventeenth century is that its decoration follows less slavishly than the Dutch the spirit of the Italian prototypes—a difference that tends to give much of the English decoration a fresher, though less exact, quality. It could be that such pieces were made by English-born potters who were uncommitted to the Italo-Flemish decorative style and were less tradition-bound than the Dutch.

1. Anthony Thwaite, "The Chronology of the Bellarmine Jug," *Connoisseur* 182 (1973): 257.
2. Ibid., 258.
3. John Hurst, "Weser Slipware from Britain and North America," in *Coppengrave—Studien zur Töpferei des 13. bis 19. Jahrhunderts in Nordwestdeutschland*, (by) Hans Georg Stephan (Hildescheim: 1981), 142; G. Elzinga and Dingeman Korf, *Vondsten uit eigen bodem*, Fries Museum Facetten 9 (Leeuwarden: Fries Museum, 1978), 12.
4. Jan Baart, "Weserware in Amsterdam" (trans. Dr. Frederick Nachod), in *Coppengrave—Studien zur Töpferei*, photographs.
5. Ibid., 139.
6. A large (42 cm) sixteenth-century dish of the Werra ware type recently appeared as the only object on the page in an advertisement in an international magazine devoted to fine ceramics. This dish is particularly intriguing since it strangely combines a somewhat primitive and carelessly applied slip decoration on rim and in *cavetto* with an intricate center design featuring the embossed coat of arms of a sixteenth-century archbishop of Cologne. (*Ceramics*, 1986, no. 2: 16.)
7. Edmund B. O'Callaghan, *Documents Relative to the Colonial History of the State of New York* (Albany: Weed, Parsons and Co., 1853-1858), 3:44.
8. Seizo Hayashiya and Henry Trubner, *Chinese Ceramics from Japanese Collections* (New York: Asia Society, 1977), 40-41.
9. C. B. van der Pijl-Ketel, ed., *The Ceramic Load of the 'Witte Leeuw' (1613)* (Amsterdam: Rijksmuseum, n.d.); Lita Solis-Cohen, "Hatcher's China from the Sea," *Maine Antique Digest* (September 1984): 18B.
10. A disturbed period in Chinese history between 1620 and 1681 during which the nation was involved in internal dissension and war, following the Manchu invasion near the end of the Ming dynasty.

16

Ceramics Found on Former New Netherland Sites

Such archaeological work as has been done on seventeenth-century trading or settlement sites along our Atlantic seaboard has at times been uneven in quality and unsystematic in focus. Occasionally, important sites have been excavated without adequate preliminary historical research or the implementation of proper techniques. Now and then sites have been destroyed without previous archaeological investigation, as in the case of Fort *Goed Hoop*, the Dutch trading settlement on the *Versche* (Connecticut) River, the site of which was destroyed partly by natural erosion and partly by public engineering works in this century.

In a paper read before a Dutch colonial symposium held at New York University on March 2, 1985, Paul R. Huey pointed out that in the late eighteenth century, interest in archaeology on Dutch sites was aroused by several Dutch artifacts recovered more or less accidentally in the course of construction activities on Manhattan. These, however, were treated merely as "quaint" reminders of the early Dutch, and no particular interest was shown (except by one individual) in their public preservation or the value they might have as measures of the material culture of an earlier time.[1] Aside from the more solid antiquarian interests of Jefferson and a few other leaders whose efforts in early archaeology were scientifically oriented, most discoveries occurred in a hit-or-miss manner, unaccompanied by any sustained plan for preservation.[2]

In the latter part of the nineteenth century, there was a notable burgeoning of enthusiasm for aboriginal site archaeology, but such historical artifacts as were found in conjunction with Indian remains were often ignored or even thrown aside. In the 1920s, Huey points out, interest in historical archaeology began to solidify, though it is still centered for the most part around sites and artifacts discovered accidentally through construction.[3] It was undoubtedly the Great Depression of the 1930s, with the historical public works projects that grew out of it, that inaugurated a recognition of the importance of historical archaeology and inspired the eventual development of better practices in preservation.

Within the last twenty-five years, an increased recognition of the significance of archaeological artifacts to the social and economic history of a people has increased activity in the field of historical archaeology and has resulted in a higher standard of professional involvement. Unquestionably, some states and municipalities have been more supportive of this research than others, and there are areas that have not been explored to the extent their historical importance deserves. Yet the outlook for this kind of work is encouraging and the results already achieved, impressive.

This recent archaeological activity has revealed an unsuspected quantity of Dutch ceramic artifacts on American seventeenth-century sites—certainly enough to correct earlier misconceptions that led our historians to underestimate the Dutch cultural impact on colonial America. Although documentary evidence of this is plentiful, the destruction in 1821 of the Dutch West India Company records makes this archaeological testimony of Dutch trading activities in America especially valuable.

Of the important seventeenth-century Dutch settlement sites located in areas formerly a part of New Netherland, only a few have been investigated archaeologically, with varying degrees of thoroughness. Those in the Albany and Manhattan areas—the earliest of the sites—have been excavated with a high degree of professional dedication and care, and these excavations can provide dependable guidelines for all further research on seventeenth-century Dutch material culture in America.

From Paul R. Huey's authoritative article, "Dutch Sites of the Seventeenth Century in Rensselaerswyck," we have a listing of the sites in the neighborhood of Albany. These are the West India Company sites—Fort Orange and areas of Broadway, State Street and South Pearl Street in downtown Albany—and the Rensselaerswyck sites, which include Schuyler Flatts, Riverside Avenue in Rensselaer, New York, and the Van Buren farm site.[4] Since Huey's article was written, two other seventeenth-century sites have come to light in Albany as a result of a large bank construction project on the corner of

South Pearl and Norton streets—the so-called Key Corp and Parking Garage sites. Excavations here have produced the remains of two seventeenth-century houses, one believed to date from the New Netherland period, an early colonial cemetery with stacked burials, and artifacts that include Dutch majolica, both Dutch and English fayence, English combed ware, and beads and other artifacts of the Indian trade. Another New Netherland site is the so-called Senate House site in Kingston, New York, in Dutch times called *Wiltwyck*.

EXCAVATION AT FORT ORANGE (ALBANY, NEW YORK)

During the winter of 1970-71, the archaeological excavation of Fort Orange, the earliest permanent settlement of the Dutch in America, was undertaken under difficult weather conditions and time pressures. That fort, built in 1624, was continuously occupied by the Dutch until 1664, in which year the English took it and occupied it until 1676, except for a period of a few months in 1673-74 when the Dutch returned. It was abandoned by the English in 1676, and they built a new fort some distance away in another part of town.

Throughout much of its existence, Fort Orange had not served merely as a military post, but had embraced within its walls an astonishing miscellany of people and structures, the latter housing West India Company officials, fur traders, artisans, and even a brewery. Archaeologists were able to establish the ownership of a number of the small buildings from extant Dutch records.

The work of excavation was undertaken in the fall of 1970 by the New York State Historic Trust, now the Office of Parks, Recreation and Historic Preservation, and was directed by Paul R. Huey. In a sense it was a milestone in American archaeology since it was the first time that an important seventeenth-century Dutch site here had been excavated with rigid professional supervision and methods. The work produced a large body of artifacts that was, in effect, a sealed packet. It is true that there had been intrusions on the site by eighteenth-century residential structures and by railway, street, and utility installations in the nineteenth and twentieth centuries, but between the time of the abandonment of Fort Orange and the erection of the first urban structure on the site, in 1794, nearly 120 years had elapsed, during which the fort had been left to turn into a mound of rubble and dirt, unused except for gardens and pastureland, with the exception of one brief period in the mid-eighteenth century when British troops were encamped there.

In the twelve years between 1664 and 1676, during most of which time the British occupied Fort Orange, there were opportunities for the accumulation of artifacts of British manufacture. However, not only did the people of Albany, being primarily Dutch, prefer Dutch goods to English goods, but also the English commercial world was not then equipped to meet the challenge of supplying the province of New York with consumer goods of the type to which it had become accustomed under Dutch rule.

A makeshift fireplace encountered by the archaeologists of Fort Orange at a level consistent with the English occupation of the fort indicates that the housekeeping of the small English garrison was spartan. This is further borne out by the dearth of English ceramic wares of the period found there.

The collection of seventeenth-century artifacts from Fort Orange constitutes an encapsulated corpus of material representing Dutch consumer goods of the second and third quarters of the seventeenth century. This virtually uncontaminated group of artifacts not only offers a criterion for isolating Dutch material from English on other American archaeological sites, but also introduces a new dimension for estimating the extent of Dutch trade with the former British colonies. This body of artifacts could prove equally valuable for analyzing material found on seventeenth-century French or Spanish sites along the eastern seaboard of America.

The ceramic artifacts recovered at Fort Orange fall into five distinct groups: (1) Dutch ceramics, (2) German salt-glazed stoneware, (3) Iberian and Italian wares, (4) Chinese porcelain, and (5) English earthenwares.

DUTCH CERAMICS

Majolica. The decorative pattern found most often on the large amount of majolica recovered at Fort Orange is the so-called Wan-li design, a motif that always indicates an early seventeenth-century settlement date when occurring on Dutch majolica (Figs. 11, 12, 28, 29). On these pieces, the rim design of stylized Chinese symbols occurs in both a medium cobalt blue on a white ground and white reserves on a very dark blue ground. The latter style may represent older wares. Center designs for dishes with this border include the bird-on-a-rock pattern, rocks and oversize flowers, and a mandarin figure. In some examples the decoration is done crudely.

There is also one large portion of a majolica plate or dish that is entirely white on its obverse side. Dishes such as these were apparently copied by Dutch potters from similar ones in Italian fayence that were imported into the Netherlands,[5] though Chinese *blanc-de-chine* porcelains made in the

Fig. 28. Dutch majolica *papkom* or porridge bowl in the popular Wan-li design, with similar sherds from Fort Orange.
(Bowl) *Albany Institute of History and Art*
(Sherds and photo) *New York State Office of Parks, Recreation and Historic Preservation*

Fukien Province in the seventeenth century may have been the prototype for both wares.

Other decorative styles for the Fort Orange majolica are the geometric (a holdover from the Gothic), the Italianate, and pseudo-naturalistic flower motifs (Pls. 1, 2, 3, 7). These majolica patterns recovered at Fort Orange are with a few exceptions represented in Dingeman Korf's book on Dutch majolica.[6] This Dutch book, for which there is no English translation, is currently the standard work on the subject. Its hand-drawn illustrations have captions so standardized in wording that the English reader can interpret much of their meaning.

Many of the majolica sherds from Fort Orange have the greenish glaze tone on the reverse side described in the discussion of majolica in chapter 13.

Fayence. As would be expected on a site as exclusively Dutch as Fort Orange, a rich collection of fayence sherds was recovered there, representative in content of Dutch ceramic manufacture during the middle years of the seventeenth century (Pls. 5, 6, 12; Figs. 30, 31). The Chinese Ming design named after the Emperor Wan-li was again found to be prominent in the fayence sherds from Fort Orange. Here it occurs on a rather fine, thin-walled type of fayence, and the pattern follows closely that used many years earlier by the makers of Dutch majolica. Other tradi-

tional Chinese designs occur here also, contributing more decorative variety than in the case of the majolica. For the most part, ceramic sherds from Fort Orange are relatively small. Among the fayence, however, there are a number of large sherds, some of which deserve comment.

One of these is a portion of a small bowl in a Ming floral and medallion design that can perhaps be called "proto-fayence" since it has features that suggest a transitional stage between majolica and fayence (Pl. 5). Its attractive decoration is applied with skill, and the glaze is the clear white expected on fine examples of fayence, but the body of the piece has a thickness and redness of paste associated with early Dutch majolica. There are likewise two nine-inch plates represented by large sherds with plain white rims and a center design in cobalt showing a house in one case (Pl. 6) and a swan in the other. Their general style is reminiscent of those Dutch fayence plates having in the center landscapes by van Frijtom, but the Fort Orange plates have a thick body, are crudely painted, and are a style of fayence believed by

Fig. 29. Dutch majolica plate with Wan-li border and bird-on-a-rock pattern, first half of the seventeenth century, with sherds from Fort Orange.
(Dish) *Albany Institute of History and Art*
(Sherds and photo) *New York State Office of Parks, Recreation and Historic Preservation*

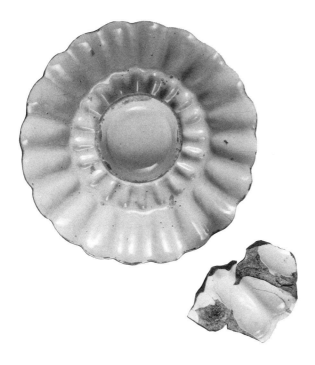

Fig. 30. This sherd from Fort Orange came from an all-white, lobed fayence dish similar to the one pictured here, which probably dates from the third quarter of the seventeenth century.
(Dish) *Crailo State Historic Site*
(Sherd and photo) *New York State Office of Parks, Recreation and Historic Preservation*

Fig. 31. The handle sherd or "ear" (*upper right*), excavated from Fort Orange, undoubtedly came from a fayence *papkom* (porridge bowl) similar to the one shown here.
(Bowl) *Crailo State Historic Site*
(Sherd and photo) *New York State Office of Parks, Recreation and Historic Preservation*

Dutch experts to have been made as early as the 1650s.

In classifying tin-glazed sherds, some American archaeologists still prefer not to distinguish between Dutch majolica and Dutch fayence (delft). The former normally occurs on American sites dating roughly from 1600 to 1660, or possibly on Indian sites of the early seventeenth century; Dutch fayence enters the scene around 1640 and continues throughout the seventeenth century. Analyses of the Fort Orange sherds indicate that the proportion of the two wares, or their very presence or absence, can provide valuable help in determining the chronology of variations in the material culture of a region, as well as furnish a yardstick for other aspects of a site.

Utility wares. The Fort Orange sherds of Dutch utility wares constitute one of the most valuable ceramic research tools yet recovered by American archaeologists from a seventeenth-century site, particularly since none of these Dutch types of ceramics, with the exception of fayence, is usually found in American museum collections.[7]

Of the utility earthenwares, the cinnamon brown, lead-glazed kind is found in great numbers at Fort

Orange, as are the green- and yellow-glazed earthenwares (all described in chapter 12). The German-derived utility types may or may not occur, since they are difficult to distinguish from Dutch earthenwares made in the same style and manner (Fig. 4). However, these latter types, whether of Dutch or German manufacture, are rare at Fort Orange.[8]

The largest number of utility earthenware sherds in the Fort Orange group is of the undecorated, cinnamon brown redware type, represented here by flat-handled skillets, pipkins in several sizes, jugs, shallow colanders, and some undetermined vessels (Pls. 4, 13-16).

An earthenware with a dark green, slightly mottled glaze and a coarse, whitish body fabric is also present in the Fort Orange sherds. This occurs in colanders and other utility dishes, though less frequently in pipkins, possibly because these vessels are frequently exposed to the heat of the fire, and it is possible that the white body cannot stand much heat.

There is another utility type with a light green glaze on one surface and a yellow glaze on the other. It is lead-glazed and has a buff body not unlike that of fayence or of the later English buff-colored earthenwares. This ware is similar to one made in England in the sixteenth and seventeenth centuries called Hampshire-Surrey ware. Finally, there is a light yellow ware with a buff body that occurs in cups, small pipkins, small milk jugs, and the like.

Tiles. The tiles used at Fort Orange, judging by the sherds recovered there, were of a common, inexpensive type. Most had ox-head corners or plain corners, usually with a small figure of a person or animal in the center. There is one example of a Chinese fretwork corner from the Flatts, but no examples of seventeenth-century polychrome tiles occur.

The Dutch ceramics on this site duplicate those being used in the Netherlands at the same period as the Fort Orange occupation, within the limitations to be expected for a middle-income population. They may be compared with those found in excavations of mid-seventeenth-century sites in Amsterdam, with the aforementioned reservations.

GERMAN SALT-GLAZED STONEWARE

The German stonewares from Fort Orange are of the Westerwald or Cologne-Frechen types exclusively, which wares have been discussed in detail in chapter 15.

The gray-and-blue Westerwald sherds are numerous and of a wide range of design motifs. They appear to represent only drinking *Krüge* that may generally be dated to the two middle quarters of the seventeenth century. Since the court records of Fort Orange and Beverwyck (the latter, post-1652) show the inhabitants of that area to have been greatly addicted to conviviality, this plethora of drinking vessels is reassuringly supportive of the documentary testimony.

Motifs found on the Fort Orange Westerwald sherds (Pl. 11) include rosettes of many kinds, sworled, incised and raised; raised friezes in arabesques; stamped and incised hearts; floral motifs; slightly anthropomorphic lions' heads in high relief; angels' heads; *Flechtwerk* (basket work); and raised, rounded moldings separating areas of design. The ends of handles are crimped under—not the later rattail types.

None of these Westerwald sherds from Fort Orange shows the touches of manganese introduced into the manufacture of that stoneware sometime later in the seventeenth century, which may indicate that its introduction was after the New Netherland period, or at least near the end of it. Two of the Westerwald sherds from this site have inscriptions. One is fragmented to "RG. 1632"; the other, incomplete at either end, "RINS • dER • HERZ • LEB."[9] Some of these German words also occur on a sherd

from the Dann site, a former Seneca village in western New York State that was occupied from 1655 to 1675.[10]

It would appear that the date in the aforementioned inscription had significance for the potters of the Westerwald district. In 1632 Siegburg, a nearby city with a distinguished potting tradition, was sacked by the Swedes during the Thirty Years' War, and the Swedish king, Gustavus Adolphus, scourge of the Rhineland, was killed in the same year. Whether either of these events accounts for the date appearing on the sherd is problematical, but it appears likely that the date is commemorative rather than indicative of the time when the piece of stoneware was made. In this connection, Bernard Rackham, in his article on German stonewares for the eleventh edition of *Encyclopaedia Britannica*, warned that "it must not always be inferred that a piece is as old as the date introduced in its decoration."[11] It should be noted, however, that the sherds from New York archaeological sites having such inscriptions and dates were recovered from early seventeenth-century levels consistent with their dates.

Sherds of Bartmann jugs with Frechen's brown-mottled glazes (see chapter 15 for a detailed discussion) were found in relatively great numbers at Fort Orange and Schuyler Flatts (Pls. 9, 10; Figs. 23, 24, 32). The earlier Cologne-type jugs differ from most of the Bartmanns at Fort Orange in having a more globular body and a more carefully delineated mask than the angular, rather repellent faces on the Frechen jugs. Some of the Fort Orange jugs, as well as some found at Schuyler Flatts, have on their medallion areas splashes of cobalt blue applied over the brown glaze.

The Frechen jugs found at the aforementioned American sites are often identical in form and decoration to those recovered through underwater archaeology from sunken wrecks of Dutch trading vessels of the same period as these sites. Two such wrecks documented in published reports are those of the *Batavia* and the *Vergulde Draeck*, both of which ships sank in western Australian waters, the former in 1629, the latter in 1656.[12] These dates coincide with the most active years of Dutch trading in America, and sherds of jugs similar to those found on these wrecks have been found at Fort Orange and the other early seventeenth-century sites in the Albany area, as well as on Indian sites in central New York State and at the *Stadthuys* site in metropolitan New York City.

Among the medallion designs on the Bartmann jugs from Fort Orange are the familiar three saltires (St. Andrew's crosses) of the arms of the city of Amsterdam (Fig. 24) and several other unidentified arms, all strikingly similar to the heraldic devices on jugs from the previously mentioned Dutch shipwrecks dating from around the middle of the seventeenth century. They are also similar to the medallion designs of Bartmann jugs found archaeologically at Jamestown (Virginia) (Fig. 32) and at early Virginia plantation sites. (Sherds from many of these plantation sites are now in the Virginia Center for Archaeological Research at Richmond, Virginia.)

Fig. 32. This *Bartmannkrug*, found in the fill of an early seventeenth-century well in Jamestown, Virginia, is typical of jugs used at Fort Orange and Schuyler Flatts. It is also representative of the jugs taken from wrecks of mid-seventeenth-century Dutch trading vessels.
Colonial National Historical Park, National Park Service

The importance of the German stoneware sherds from Fort Orange becomes more obvious when it is considered that among European seventeenth-century ceramics, these have been exposed to rigid review and classification over a long period of time and thus can serve as a dependable dating yardstick for Dutch-American sites. The German stoneware sherds found at Fort Orange firmly support the mid-seventeenth-century dating of that site and give clues to some of the cultural attitudes of its inhabitants.

IBERIAN AND ITALIAN WARES

Iberian tin-glazed earthenwares are sparsely represented in the Fort Orange sherds, a situation that may appear strange in view of the extensive contacts at that time between the Dutch and the Spanish in the Caribbean and elsewhere. We know from the public records of New Netherland that in the 1640s privateering out of New Amsterdam against the Spanish was an important Dutch enterprise and that several ships were engaged in this, one of the most active being the frigate *La Garce*, Willem Blauvelt, master. This ship was owned by Dutchmen from Manhattan and Fort Orange, and the director and council of New Netherland commissioned her "to go privateering from here to the West Indies" on June 1, 1644. There is evidence that she had been engaged in this kind of activity for several years prior to this. In the commission, it is stated that the crew of *La Garce* had earlier in the year, "with the help of God, by force of arms," brought into the harbor at New Amsterdam two Spanish barks, one taken in the Caribbean, the other intercepted on a course from Spain to Guatemala. These were declared "good prizes" and their Spanish owners debarred from further claim to them or their cargoes.[13]

In 1646, Blauvelt and his crew took the bark *San Antonio de la Havana*, which was on a course from Havana to Campeche (in Yucatan), and brought it into New Amsterdam in July of that year.[14] In 1648, the master and crew of *La Garce* took another Spanish ship in the Bay of Campeche, laden with "piece goods." They apparently renamed her *De Hoop* before bringing her to New Amsterdam, but because of the peace subsequently declared between the two nations, the prize status of *De Hoop* was challenged in New Netherland courts and a compromise reached with her owners.[15]

The director and council of New Netherland, on June 20, 1647, ordered the yachts *De Liefde* and *De Kath* to be chartered as privateers against the Spaniards.[16] Of these, *De Liefde* was a vessel of fifty tons burden and carried a crew of sixteen.[17] The following year the council minutes record that *De Kath* brought into New Amsterdam the Spanish bark *Nuestra Señora del Rosario* as prize.[18]

These examples of Dutch privateering out of New Netherland are cited out of many to show the nature of these operations and the opportunities they produced for Spanish ceramics to reach New Netherland. There was also constant trading between the two countries during intervals of peace.

Dutch tin-glazed earthenware of the seventeenth century, whether majolica or fayence, always has a pure white glaze since Dutch potters did not skimp on the amount of tin oxide used. Iberian potters, however, were more conservative with the expensive commodity. This resulted in a cream white glaze rather than a pure white one, and therefore when a tin-glazed sherd from an eastern seaboard site shows this cream tone, the possibility that it is of Spanish or Portuguese provenance should be considered.

One Iberian sherd from Fort Orange is worthy of special notice—about one-third of a small cup, thinly potted and with a very white glaze and buff body (Fig. 33). This piece is attractively decorated in a cobalt blue floral motif and is edged below the rim with a lace design in black. This design was employed in the seventeenth century by potters in Portugal, in Talavera de la Reina, Spain, and in Puebla, Mexico. John Goggin called the latter "Puebla Polychrome" and noted that it was exported widely to the Caribbean area,[19] whence this cup might easily have reached New Netherland.[20] The *loza fina*, or high-quality ware of Puebla, has a pure white glaze, while the cheaper wares made there often have a cream-colored glaze.

Fig. 33. Fayence cup, mid-seventeenth century. This thin-walled cup with black-lace decoration may be of either Iberian or Mexican (Puebla) origin. It was found at Fort Orange.
New York State Office of Parks, Recreation and Historic Preservation.

Many fragments of Spanish olive jars were found at Fort Orange.

Although Portuguese tin-glazed earthenware (majolica) occurs with frequency on seventeenth-century archaeological sites in Massachusetts and Virginia,[21] it has not been identified in the up-river Albany area. That found in both Massachusetts and Virginia has a variant of the Wan-li border, but often this is carelessly applied and departs much more widely from the Chinese prototype than does the same basic design on Dutch and English majolica.

Italian marbleized slipware was recovered from Fort Orange, though in small quantity (Fig. 25).

ORIENTAL PORCELAINS

Chinese export porcelain. Compared with other non-Dutch ceramics, little Chinese porcelain was found at the Fort Orange site, and that discovered was difficult to attribute to specific time periods. A few small sherds appear to be of the late Ming dynasty or of the Transition Period that followed, but examples of Chinese porcelain in the Wan-li pattern of the so-called *Kraakporselein,* so valued in the Netherlands, have not been identified among the Fort Orange fragments.

The lack of Chinese porcelain on this site is probably due primarily to the fact that the entire period of the Dutch occupation of Fort Orange coincided with the Chinese civil wars and the Transition Period in Chinese history. Of this, Suzanne G. Valenstein, an American authority on Chinese porcelain, says: "For the sake of providing a working date, the 'Transition Period' in Chinese ceramics is considered to have started with the death of the Wan-li emperor in 1620. It spanned the changeover from the Ming to the Ch'ing Dynasty in 1644 and extended to the arrival of Ts'ang Ying-hsüan as director of the imperial [porcelain] factories at Ching-te Chen in 1681 or 1683."[22] Since Fort Orange was built in 1624 and given up finally by the Dutch in 1674, it can be seen how neatly these dates coincide. Earlier, R. L. Hobson, an English authority on Chinese porcelain, had written, ". . . we are left to infer that during the death struggles of the old dynasty [the Ming] and the establishment of the Manchu Tartars on the throne the work at the Imperial factory was virtually suspended."[23]

Current opinion seems to be that in spite of the upheaval in China at this time, quite fine porcelain continued to be made and even exported to Europe and southeastern and western Asia in the Transition Period. This view is supported by the findings from shipwrecks salvaged within recent years, which have produced new data on the wares of the Transition Period that have caused important museums throughout the world to change their dating guidelines for porcelain of that time. On the other hand, the civil wars certainly curtailed the quantity of ceramics produced and exported to the West. Possible confirmation of this may be found in a letter that the sister of Jeremias van Rensselaer (director of the *colonie* of Rensselaerswyck) wrote her brother after he asked her to buy him some household goods in Amsterdam. "I had much trouble in procuring the small table plates," she wrote, "as not many are being made."[24] This was in 1662. Since at this time the fayence factories in Delft and elsewhere in the Netherlands were producing at full capacity and small plates in fayence would not have been difficult to find, this must refer to porcelain plates.

Sherds of Ming porcelain are much more prevalent on early Virginia sites than on early Dutch sites in New York; indeed, they are found in considerable numbers on the southern sites dating from the 1630s, and "there is . . . substantial circumstantial evidence to suggest that the Dutch brought over the early Chinese ceramics found in the James River basin."[25] The difference in the quantity of Chinese ceramics found in the two areas may rest largely on a chronological reason. Many sherds found in Virginia date from the last years of the Ming dynasty or from the early part of the Transition Period, before the civil wars in China seriously interrupted production. At this time, the Dutch at Fort Orange and Manhattan were not yet wealthy enough to afford porcelains, and by the time their prosperity had increased to the point where they were—in the 1650s and 1660s—China's ceramic industry and trade had been seriously curtailed.

Japanese porcelain. No traces of Japanese porcelain, which was being imported into the Netherlands in large quantities at this period, were found at Fort Orange, nor has any been found archaeologically at other seventeenth-century sites in New York State, as far as this author knows.

ENGLISH CERAMICS

The number of seventeenth-century English sherds from Fort Orange that can be identified with certainty is minimal. They include a few gravel-tempered earthenwares and a portion of a small redware pot that does not resemble the characteristic Dutch redware found there.

Judging by the dearth of English artifacts recovered from seventeenth-century layers at Fort Orange, it would appear that only a rudimentary type of military mess ever existed in the fort. This reasoning is bolstered by the discovery of a crude fireplace constructed of loose bricks on the floor of a room in one of the houses, suggesting that the barracks cooking done there was on a primitive level. However, a section of wine bottle with the name "F. Louelace" scratched on it was found at Fort Orange. Francis Lovelace was the English governor of New York, 1668-1674.

SCHUYLER FLATTS

Schuyler Flatts, three or four miles north of Fort Orange on the Hudson River, was originally called *de Groote Vlacte* by the Dutch. It came to be considered one of the most desirable farms in the *colonie* of Rensselaerswyck, not only because of its fertile alluvial soil, but also because it lay athwart one of the principal routes along which the Indians brought their furs to Fort Orange. Here the Indians could be intercepted before they reached the fort, and the cream of the peltries could be skimmed off.

As far as can now be learned, the first tenant-in-residence of the farm on the great flat was Adriaen vander Donck, hired by Kiliaen van Rensselaer as *schout*[26] for Rensselaerswyck in 1641. Vander Donck came to the *colonie* in the summer of that year and, instead of settling on a location near Fort Orange, as the patroon intended him to, established himself without the patroon's permission on *de Groote Vlacte*, which lay just north of the farm occupied by Cornelis Anthonisz van Slyck.[27] However, because of the patroon's displeasure at his establishing his residence so far from Fort Orange, vander Donck left the Flatts in 1643, and the management of that important farm was then turned over to Arent van Curler, a kinsman of the patroon. It was probably van Curler who, on February 9, 1643, engaged Rutger Jacobsz as foreman for the farm,[28] and it appears that he also intended to give tenancy of the Flatts to Jean Labatie, a French carpenter. The patroon, however, was not in favor of this,[29] and van Laer indicates that, instead, Labatie at this time left the patroon's service.[30]

The Flatts was now the northernmost farm in the *colonie*, on the west side of the Hudson River, and in 1643 van Curler built a small house there and contracted for the construction of a large combined farmhouse and barn.[31] According to van Laer, in 1647 van Curler obtained a six-year lease of the Flatts, but two years later this was transferred to Jacob Jansz, of Stoutenburch.[32] By 1668 Jeremias van Rensselaer, then-director of Rensselaerswyck, was writing thus of the old place: "On the Vlackte the house has caved in and [must be] totally repaired. I can get no good tenant for it, so that it [stands] empty."[33]

The tenant who eventually took over the Flatts was Ryckert van Rensselaer, brother of Jeremias, but in 1670 he returned to the Netherlands. On June 22, 1672, the Flatts was sold to Philip Pieterse Schuyler, for a total of 8,000 guilders.[34] From that time it has been known as Schuyler Flatts, and it was continuously occupied by members of the Schuyler family until well into the twentieth century.

Throughout the seventeenth century, this place was an active center for trade with both the Indians from the Mohawk Valley and the French in Canada. Toward the end of the century, the Flatts was sometimes used as a gathering point for military sorties against the latter nation. Thus, a large and motley company composed of traders, Indians, soldiers, Blacks, and Dutch settlers passed constantly through its palisaded precincts and along the stretch of river in front of its gates, making it one of the busiest spots in all of New Netherland, in spite of its rural location. The historical significance of this site can well be imagined.

The Dutch artifacts recovered at Schuyler Flatts closely parallel those from corresponding levels at Fort Orange though perhaps they tend to be slightly more sophisticated in quality, as might be expected from a site occupied by men as cosmopolitan for the time and place as vander Donck, van Curler, Ryckert van Rensselaer, and Philip Pieterse Schuyler.

CERAMICS AT THE FLATTS

Specific patterns occurring in the Westerwald sherds from the Flatts are angels' heads in relief, surrounded by large halos; a frieze with the satanic head of a bearded man in relief; another frieze giving the story of the Prodigal Son; the arms of Amsterdam; a design of four incised hearts with points converging on a centered rosette; latticework patterns; small circular medallions and raised, sworled rosettes; and carefully molded raised borders for dividing areas of design. There is at least one sherd in the *Netzornament* style (see chapter 15).[35]

Dated and inscribed Westerwald sherds from the Flatts include one with the incomplete inscription, "KVS•1632•I," and another showing only the symbols ":LV:." Ivor Noël Hume, in a book on Virginia archaeology, shows an illustration of two dated Westerwald sherds, one from Virginia, with the partial inscription, "KVS•1632•ICH," and the other from Frankfurt, Germany, having "KVS•1632," preceded by illegible letters.[36]

Frechen stoneware jugs from the Flatts are represented by tigerware sherds with unusually large dark brown spots and green-tinted areas of glaze, masks, and medallions showing armorial devices or massed rosettes (Figs. 23, 24). The latter are virtually identical to those on jug fragments from the ship *Batavia*, wrecked in 1629, as well as to many from the *Vergulde Draeck*, wrecked in 1656. A large fragment of a globular Cologne-type jug has on it the arms of Cologne.

Sherds of Dutch majolica and fayence from the Flatts display the same early patterns of decoration as those found at Fort Orange, and the utility wares were apparently much the same also, with the possible exception of the German-type slipwares, which have not been recovered from the Flatts. There are, however, five or six small sherds, all apparently from the same dish, that appear to be Spanish majolica, though it is not possible to establish their decorative pattern with any certainty.

VAN BUREN SITE

The Van Buren site, an early farmstead of the Dutch near Albany, has as yet been only tentatively explored but has already produced significant sherds of early Dutch majolica, fayence, and German stoneware, as well as pieces of utility wares corresponding to types found at Fort Orange. A Westerwald sherd from this site has an interesting double-eagle as its decorative motif, while another bears the partial inscription, "ICK•AVS," the first three letters appearing to form the end of a longer word. Examples of carefully molded, complex medallions from Bartmann jugs were also recovered here (Fig. 24). One of these consists of an oval shield bearing a coat of arms that is superimposed on a larger rosetted medallion—an unusual arrangement. Several of the medallions from the Van Buren site Bartmann jugs have the blue wash mentioned earlier in connection with those from Fort Orange, and which, in this writer's opinion, reflects a fairly early date in the seventeenth century.

ALBANY SITES

The Albany street sites on Huey's list produced some typical early seventeenth-century artifacts and ceramic sherds, but most of the material from these sites may be dated later in the century. This is undoubtedly because these areas were not built upon nor inhabited until the 1650s, later than the sites previously discussed.

KINGSTON-ESOPUS AREA

The settlements at Wiltwyck (Kingston) and Esopus, established later than that at Fort Orange because of Indian activities and Indian land ownership, lay about halfway between Fort Orange and Manhattan and thus occupied a strategic position in the communication between the two. They also furnished a useful agricultural resource and represented another active station in the fur trade of the Dutch. Archaeological material recovered from that area has not as yet been fully analyzed, but it is known to include some very early Dutch artifacts.

DUTCH SITES ON MANHATTAN

New Amsterdam, occupying the lower tip of Manhattan Island, was the West India Company's administrative center for the province of New Netherland and the place of residence for the director general. Since it was a heavily populated and busy commercial area, there can be no doubt that a rich detritus of artifactual material from the Dutch period remains today beneath and between the mammoth buildings.

Within the past ten years, progress has been made in tapping this archaeological and cultural resource, and in the last five years a substantial amount of seventeenth-century Dutch material has been recovered from several sites on lower Manhattan. Of these, the three producing the largest number of Dutch artifacts are the *Stadthuys* site (excavation directed by Nan Rothschild and Diana Wall), the Hanover Square site (directed by Rothschild, Wall, and Arnold Pickman), and the Broad Street site (directed by Joel Grossman). The *Stadthuys* and Broad Street sites are on fast land, the Hanover Square site on landfill. Two other landfill sites, Barclay's Bank (excavation directed by Terry Klein) and 175 Water Street (excavation directed by Joan Geismar), produced smaller quantities of Dutch material.[37] The intensive land use at these sites, both above and below ground for the past three centuries, and the many difficulties and distractions inherent in working under metropolitan conditions make these Manhattan excavations a notable accomplishment in the field of urban archaeology.

The seventeenth-century artifacts found on the Manhattan sites are generally similar in type, and at times identical, to many from Fort Orange and Schuyler Flatts. The one deviation from the pattern found in the upper Hudson sherds occurred at the Broad Street site, where the ceramic design motif known as the Wan-li pattern was absent, though the pomegranate-and-grape pattern (Pl. 3), contemporaneous on Dutch majolica with the Wan-li, was found there. The puzzle here lies in the fact that on the upper Hudson sites the number of majolica sherds with the Wan-li design was substantial, while the pomegranate occurred on only one or two sherds. On other Manhattan sites the Wan-li motif was present.[38]

It is not known to what extent early seventeenth-century Dutch artifacts have been recovered from sites on Long Island and Staten Island.

The Dutch ceramics and other artifacts recovered at the Manhattan sites fall within the same chronological period as those from Fort Orange and the Flatts, and, as in the case of the latter sites, there is no question that they were made in Dutch or other European factories and brought to New Netherland through Dutch commercial activities. Therefore, these artifacts from the two most active Dutch settlement areas in seventeenth-century America now constitute a body of Dutch evidence that henceforth can be used as a standard of comparison by archaeol-

ogists working in other geographical areas. This material has already been thus employed by prominent archaeologists and archivists from the Netherlands.

FORT *GOED HOOP* ON THE *VERSCHE* (CONNECTICUT) RIVER

The site of Fort *Goed Hoop*, established by the Dutch in 1633 on the Connecticut River at the present site of Hartford (at the mouth of the Park River), appears now to be totally destroyed. In 1981 an enquiry into the fate of this important early Dutch site produced information from the archaeologist who had prepared the archaeological impact statement for the Park River flood protection project in 1976. The site had been well known long after the abandonment of the fort, and it had remained undisturbed by the nineteenth-century urban sprawl of Hartford. However, the meandering and flooding of the Connecticut River evidently eradicated any trace of the site, as indicated by successive maps. The original conduit outfall, flood protection barriers, Highway I-91 construction, and the river's continued erosion have now permanently destroyed the site. Excavations south of the known site location produced no artifactual evidence of any early historic occupation.[39]

THE DUTCH SOUTH (DELAWARE) RIVER SETTLEMENTS

Although several persons have responded helpfully to enquiries about archaeological work at the so-called South River Dutch settlement sites in Delaware, New Jersey, and Pennsylvania, in most cases it has not proven possible to obtain specific data on the exact nature and extent of the explorations made or the artifacts recovered.[40]

The Dutch had undoubtedly been trading with the Algonkian tribes of the Delaware (South) River area since 1609, but had made no settlements there until 1624, when some members of the group of Walloon refugees that came over in that year were placed at a location called *Hooghe Eylandt* (High Island, now Burlington Island), opposite the present city of Burlington, New Jersey. The Dutch version of the island's Indian name was Matinneconck, spelled with many variants.

In 1891 Charles Conrad Abbott, a doctor of medicine and curator of the Department of American Archaeology of the University of Pennsylvania Museum, found Dutch yellow clinker bricks, pipes, and other artifacts that he believed to be of Dutch provenance on Burlington Island.[41] In the accounts of Abbott's findings no mention is made of ceramic dishes, then often considered merely women's "crockery" and ignored, as they may have been here. Subsequently, according to Weslager, this Burlington Island site was destroyed by dredging operations.[42]

When, in 1626, anticipating possible uprisings of the native Americans, the Dutch withdrew the Walloon families living at Fort Orange and on the Connecticut (*Versche*) River to the newly purchased Manhattan Island, they also removed the group from *Hooghe Eylandt*. Yet in the same year they established a trading post that they named Fort Nassau on the east bank of the South River, between two creeks, the *Timmerkil* on the north and the *Verkeerdekil* on the south. Today the former of these is known as Newton Creek, the latter, as Big Timber Creek, and Gloucester City, New Jersey, now covers the site of the former Dutch fort. In 1852 an exploration of this general site was undertaken jointly by the New Jersey and Pennsylvania Historical Societies, with inconclusive findings. However, Edward Armstrong, one of the participants in the project, wrote later in a paper that Dutch bricks "with letters upon them" were found, along with Indian artifacts. He recommended further search.[43]

Swanendael, a Dutch patroonship, was established near the mouth of Delaware Bay in 1631, on the site of the present Lewes, Delaware, and in 1632 an Indian massacre took place there. In 1634 the West India Company purchased *Swanendael* from its proprietors. Later (1659) this location was known as the *Hoerenkil*.

Peter Minuit, formerly in the employ of the Dutch West India Company but now working for the Swedish South Company, led an expedition to the South River in 1638 and built Fort Christina on its west side, at the present site of Wilmington, Delaware. This was some miles down the river from, and west of, Fort Nassau, and the Swedes were now in a position to intercept much of the Indian trade from the west formerly enjoyed by the Dutch. From this time there was frequent friction between the Dutch and the Swedes.

Within the present boundaries of the city of Philadelphia, Pennsylvania, there were two early Dutch sites, one on Tinicum Island on the west side of the Delaware River, and another, *Beversreede*, about three miles up the Schuylkill from its mouth. The Swedes built a trading post, Fort *Nya Korsholm*, on the very threshold of *Beversreede*, and bitter confrontations between the two nations were frequent there. The Dutch abandoned *Beversreede* at the same time that they gave up Fort Nassau.

The Tinicum Island site (called New Gothenborg by the Swedes), was a Swedish settlement before it came into the hands of the Dutch. Here, in 1643, Johan Printz, director of the Swedish settlements on the South (Delaware) River, established a fort and home. The first dwelling built by Printz burned two years later, at which time another commodious house, often referred to as *Printzhof*, was constructed. Although it was formerly stated that this two-story structure was built of bricks transported from Sweden, current opinion is that it was probably built in the Swedish manner, of squared logs, with only fireplaces and chimneys of brick.[44] It is said to have burned shortly after 1800.[45]

After a somewhat stormy career of confrontation with the Dutch, who claimed the territory occupied by the Swedes, Printz, with his family, returned to Sweden in 1653. By 1655 the Dutch were in control of the South River, and by 1656 the former Swedish fort on Tinicum Island was garrisoned by Dutch soldiers—an occupation that continued until the English took over the region in 1664.

The site of *Printzhof* was excavated in 1930 and, more recently, in 1976 and 1985. Artifacts recovered in the course of these excavations are currently (1986) housed in the American Swedish Historical Society in Philadelphia; at West Chester University in West Chester, Pennsylvania; and at the Museum of the University of Pennsylvania in Philadelphia.[46] It has not been possible to obtain information on the exact nature of the ceramic artifacts recovered at *Printzhof*. Considering, however, the extent of Dutch trade with the Swedes on the Delaware, even before the Dutch occupation of the Tinicum site, a high percentage of Dutch ceramics might be expected to have been found there.

In order to cope with the Swedish threat to Dutch trade, Stuyvesant, playing a leapfrog game, abandoned Fort Nassau in 1651 and removed its cannon and other appurtenances to a new site on the west side of the river, naming the new place Fort Casimir. This was below Fort Christina on the river, and impeded the Swedes' access to the bay. Fort Casimir was taken over from the Dutch West India Company in 1656 by the Burgomasters of the city of Amsterdam, who renamed it New Amstel. Under the English, in 1664 it became New Castle, Delaware.

Letters of enquiry concerning archaeological activity on early Dutch sites in Delaware produced the information that though very few of these have been located archaeologically, there are two near Lewes—the "Old House" and the de Vries palisade—that were excavated by the Sussex Society for Archaeology during 1956 and 1962. Artifacts recovered have not been kept together, though some are now in the Island Field Museum. Much of the de Vries palisade area has been a graveyard for many years, and so was not explored archaeologically, though it was possible to trace portions of the palisaded wall.[47]

In 1986, Edward F. Heite and Louise B. Heite, Delaware archaeologists in the employ of the Trustees of New Castle Commons, made a test excavation on the sandy point of land in New Castle that was the site of Fort Casimir. From a small test pit on the fort site the Heites recovered significant sherds of Dutch majolica, Dutch utility wares, and German drinking vessels such as were widely distributed by the Dutch through their trade. All of the Dutch material dated from the middle years of the seventeenth century.[48]

Pavonia, the earliest settlement in northern New Jersey, was a patroonship founded by Michiel de Pauw in 1630, which passed into the ownership of the Dutch West India Company in 1634. It embraced a large area in the vicinity of the present Jersey City, Hoboken, and Staten Island, and was later the scene of serious Indian uprisings, largely as a result of Governor Kieft's ineptitude and unfortunate character. Whether any extensive archaeological investigation of the early Dutch site has been made there the author has been unable to determine.

DUTCH CERAMICS ON INDIAN SITES

Although archaeological research conducted on Indian sites is not within the scope of this book, it may still be useful to call attention to the presence of sixteenth- and early seventeenth-century European ceramics on many of these.[49] The western and central New York contact period sites and those of the Mohawk Iroquois, farther east, are particularly rich in European ceramic sherds, and more of these are coming to light as early contact period villages are further explored (Figs. 19, 20, 21).

Sometimes chronological considerations affect the incidence of specific ceramic types found on Indian sites. For example, the German Weser ware (discussed in chapter 15), distributed widely by the Dutch at one time, was not found at Fort Orange or Schuyler Flatts, nor apparently at Dutch sites on Manhattan (except possibly at the Broad Street site), presumably because its importation into Amsterdam ceased after 1620.[50] It has, however, been found on Indian sites in New York State. Of this, James W. Bradley and Monte Bennett, in a recent article, have this to say:

> Examples of Weser ware have been recovered from the Pompey Centre site (Onondaga Iroquois), located south of Syracuse, New York, and the Cameron site (Oneida Iro-

quois) located approximately twenty miles east in Munnsville, New York. The dates given for each site are drawn from a reconstructed sequence of sites based on artifactual trends, settlement pattern and correlation with the documentary record.[51]

According to the authors of this article, the Pompey Centre site dates from around 1600 to 1620, while the Cameron site is dated around 1600.

Dutch majolica and Dutch-distributed German stoneware, as well as sherds of early Dutch utility wares, occur frequently on New York Indian sites and on those of other areas formerly a part of New Netherland, or in places where the Dutch carried on an active fur trade. Barry C. Kent of the State Museum of Pennsylvania, in a recent letter to the author, wrote: "A fair number of [Dutch ceramics] have been excavated from Indian sites along the Susquehanna. However, there are none from Indian sites along the Delaware." Considering the extent of Dutch fur-trading activity on the Delaware in the seventeenth century, this last circumstance is puzzling.

Illustrations in Kent's book on the Indians of the Susquehanna Valley show various European artifacts, some of which are undoubtedly of Dutch provenance and distribution. Specifically, figures 73-77 illustrate ceramic artifacts closely resembling some found at Fort Orange, Schuyler Flatts, and at Indian sites in New York.[52]

Archaeological work directed by Dean Snow of the State University of New York at Albany in the summer of 1984 recovered a few examples of Dutch majolica and early green-glazed, white-bodied Dutch utility ware from the Naylor site, an Indian village on the Mohawk River estimated to have a mean date of 1635.

Worked gaming counters of what appears to be Spanish majolica were found on an Indian site in central New York, and numerous examples of French *faïence* and French utility ceramics have been recovered from Indian village sites in that area.

DUTCH CERAMICS ON NON-DUTCH SITES IN AMERICA

Dutch ceramics and other Dutch artifacts, as well as types of Dutch-distributed German and Italian wares, have been found on sites lying within the former non-Dutch colonies, from the Acadian sites in Maine to Spanish sites in Florida. Many years ago, archaeologists working at Jamestown correctly identified Dutch objects found there, and since that time numbers of Dutch artifacts have been recovered from several sites in Virginia and Maryland. Some archaeologists have assumed that these were brought here in ships of the countries that owned the respective colonies in the seventeenth century. There is now no way of either proving or disproving this. In view, however, of abundant documentary evidence that at that time the people of these colonies had direct and sustained commercial contacts with Dutch trading ships, it appears unlikely that they would have had to import Dutch ceramics or other Dutch goods from England, France, or Spain. We must conclude, therefore, that most Dutch artifacts now found on North American sites were brought there in Dutch bottoms.

Notes - Chapter 16

1. Paul R. Huey, "Historical and Archaeological Research and Research Questions on Seventeenth Century Dutch New Netherland" (Paper read at Colonial Dutch Symposium, New York University, March 2, 1985), 6-7.
2. Ibid., 8.
3. Ibid., 10-11.
4. Huey, "Dutch Sites of the Seventeenth Century in Rensselaerswyck," in *The Scope of Historical Archaeology: Essays in Honor of John L. Cotter,* ed. David G. Orr and Daniel G. Crozier (Philadelphia: Temple University, 1984), 63-85. See also Huey, "Archaeological Excavations in the Site of Fort Orange, a Dutch West India Company Trading Fort Built in 1624," *Bulletin, KNOB* (Royal Dutch Antiquarian Society) 84 (June 1985): 68.
5. Jan Baart, "Ceramiche italiane rinvenute in Olanda e le prime imitazioni olandesi" (trans. Melinda Yates), in *Atti, XVI Convegno Internazionale della Ceramica* (Albisola, Italy: Centro Ligure per la Storia della Ceramica, 1983), 164.
6. Dingeman Korf, *Nederlandse majolica,* 5th ed. (Haarlem: De Haan, 1981).
7. The Albany Institute of History and Art has recently acquired a collection of seventeenth-century Dutch majolica and lead-glazed utility wares.
8. Weser ware, a German earthenware widely distributed by the Dutch in the sixteenth and early seventeenth centuries, was apparently not found at Fort Orange, perhaps because it had ceased to be imported into Amsterdam prior to the settlement of Fort Orange. However, we learn from an article by James W. Bradley and Monte Bennett ("Two Occurrences of Weser Slipware from Early Seventeenth Century Iroquois Sites in New York State," *Post-Medieval Archaeology* 18 (1984): 301-5) that examples of Weser ware have been recovered from the Pompey Centre site in New York State (an Onondaga Iroquois village south of Syracuse) and from the Cameron site (Oneida Iroquois village, east of Munnsville). The first of these sites has been dated ca. 1600-1620, the second, ca. 1600. Werra ware, another German type distributed by the Dutch, is represented by only a few small sherds, and Wanfried ware, apparently not at all. (See chapter 15 for a discussion of these German earthenwares.)
9. Ivor Noël Hume, in *A Guide to Artifacts of Colonial America* ([New York: Alfred A. Knopf, 1970], 281) describes a sherd from a Virginia site (post-1644) having a medallion with the fragmented inscription, "IVS•1632•ICH•BR•." It may be that this supplies another portion of this incomplete inscription from Fort Orange.
10. Information from Paul R. Huey.
11. *Encyclopaedia Britannica,* 11th ed., 5:740a.
12. Myra Stanbury, comp., *Batavia Catalog* (Perth, Australia: Western Australian Museum, 1974); Jeremy N. Green, ed., *The Loss of the 'Verenigde Oostindische Compagnie Jacht Vergulde Draeck,' Western Australia, 1656,* BAR Supplementary Series 36, no. 1 (Oxford: 1977), 1:95-156.
13. *New York Historical Manuscripts: Dutch,* vol. 4, *Council Minutes, 1638-1649,* ed. Kenneth Scott and Kenn Stryker-Rodda, and trans. Arnold J. F. van Laer (Baltimore: Genealogical Publishing Co., 1974), 219-20.
14. Ibid., 335-36.
15. Ibid., 605-6.
16. Ibid., 379.
17. *New York Historical Manuscripts: Dutch,* vol. 3, *Register of the Provincial Secretary of New Netherland, 1648-1660,* ed. Kenneth Scott and Kenn Stryker-Rodda, and trans. Arnold J. F. van Laer (Baltimore: Genealogical Publishing Co., 1974), 57.
18. *New York Historical Manuscripts: Dutch,* 4:528-29.
19. John M. Goggin, *Spanish Majolica in the New World,* in Yale University Publications in Archaeology, no. 72 (New Haven: Yale University Press, 1968), 191.
20. This sherd and several others from Fort Orange and Schuyler Flatts singled out for special comment in this chapter are currently on exhibit at Crailo State Historic Site, Rensselaer, New York, operated by the New York State Office of Parks, Recreation and Historic Preservation.
21. By the middle of the seventeenth century, New England merchants had established a trade with Portugal's so-called Wine Islands and with Lisbon itself, all quite independent of England. It is likely that this trade, and not that with the Dutch, accounts for the relatively large quantity of Portuguese ceramics found in the Boston area. There is documentary evidence, too, that by the late 1620s, Portuguese ships were bringing cargoes of salt to Boston, and perhaps also to Virginia.
22. Suzanne G. Valenstein, *A Handbook of Chinese Ceramics* (New York: Metropolitan Museum of Art, 1975), 168.
23. R. L. Hobson, *Chinese Pottery and Porcelain* (1915; reprint [2 vols. in 1], New York: Dover Publications, 1976), 2:86.
24. Jeremias van Rensselaer, *Correspondence,* ed. and trans. Arnold J. F. van Laer (Albany: University of the State of New York, 1932), 291.
25. Julia B. Curtis, "Chinese Ceramics and the Dutch Connection in Early Seventeenth Century Virginia," *Vereniging van vrienden der Aziatische kunst Amsterdam, Mededelingenblad* 15 (February 1985): 9.
26. This office entailed duties similar to those of a sheriff, as well as certain magisterial duties.
27. Arnold J. F. van Laer, ed. and trans., *Van Rensselaer Bowier Manuscripts* (Albany: University of the State of New York, 1908), 616-17.
28. Ibid., 812.
29. Ibid., 660, 666.
30. Ibid., 813.

31. Dutch Settlers Society of Albany, *Yearbook* 3 (1927-1928): 21-22.
32. Van Laer, *Van Rensselaer Bowier Manuscripts*, 817.
33. Van Rensselaer, *Correspondence*, 407.
34. George W. Schuyler, *Colonial New York* (New York: Charles Scribner's Sons, 1885), 1:158; Van Rensselaer, *Correspondence*, 450.
35. A sherd of this type was recovered from the *Stadthuys* site in New York City (Fig. 22).
36. Noël Hume, *All the Best Rubbish* (New York: Harper and Row, 1974), 109.
37. Information on the Manhattan sites was given to me by Nan Rothschild.
38. Information from Paul R. Huey.
39. Roger W. Moeller, letter to R. Arthur Johnson, September 19, 1981. Copy courtesy of Mr. Johnson.
40. For much of the material in this section the author is indebted to Dr. Charles T. Gehring, director of the New Netherland Project of the New York State Library.
41. Lucy L. Aiello, "Burlington Island," *New Jersey History* 91 (1973): 24-25.
42. Clinton Alfred Weslager in collaboration with Arthur Roy Dunlap, *Dutch Explorers, Traders and Settlers in the Delaware Valley, 1609-1664* (Philadelphia: University of Pennsylvania Press, 1961), 81.
43. Ibid., 124-25.
44. Amandus Johnson, *The Swedish Settlements on the Delaware, 1638-1664* (Baltimore: Genealogical Publishing Co., 1969), 1:348.
45. Henry D. Paxson, *Sketch and Map of a Trip from Philadelphia to Tinicum Island, Delaware County, Pennsylvania* (Philadelphia: George H. Buchanan Co., 1926), 107.
46. Information supplied by Barry C. Kent of the State Museum of Pennsylvania and Marshall J. Becker of the University of Pennsylvania.
47. Alice H. Guerrant, letters to the author, 1981 and 1983.
48. Edward F. Heite and Louise B. Heite, "Report of Phase I Archaeological and Historical Investigation at the Site of Fort Casimir, New Castle, Delaware" (Report prepared for Trustees of New Castle Commons, Delaware, September 1986).
49. The Rochester Museum and Science Center, Rochester, New York, has an outstanding collection of Dutch ceramics from Indian sites.
50. Baart, "Weserware in Amsterdam" (trans. Dr. Frederick Nachod), in *Coppengrave—Studien zur Töpferei des 13. bis 19. Jahrhunderts in Nordwestdeutschland*, (by) Hans Georg Stephan (Hildescheim: 1981), 139.
51. Bradley and Bennett, "Two Occurrences of Weser Slipware," 301-5.
52. Barry C. Kent, *Susquehanna's Indians* (Harrisburg: Pennsylvania Historical Museum, 1984).

Postscript

From earliest times trade has been the device by which peoples have improved their material culture and acquired the necessities for sustenance and comfort that they could not produce for themselves. Throughout history, certain nations have demonstrated a greater than ordinary talent for trading and through this aptitude have enriched their people.

In antiquity, traders of the Middle East penetrated to China and remote parts of Asia in search of useful or exotic products, while China itself, it is now believed, traded widely in eastern waters with surprisingly large vessels. Later, the Phoenicians led in the trade of the then-known world, followed in Renaissance times by the Italians and Portuguese. By the sixteenth century, the Dutch, who had for a long time maintained their national existence by trade with other nations, through a burgeoning nautical inventiveness and skill, embarked on a program of trading that in the following century would make them masters of world commerce.

All of this is well known and has often been remarked upon. Less publicized is the Dutch success in the seventeenth century at capturing the trade of the American colonies belonging to their neighbors. The story of this is yet to be related adequately by English or American academic historians, and indeed to understand the extent of this trade it would be necessary to explore voluminous Dutch archival material at its source. Yet even without this, a modicum of research will reveal that the Dutch trade with all parts of colonial America went far beyond what our English-language historians have indicated. These historians have been hampered not only by language difficulties, but also by chauvinistic prejudices toward the English. On the other hand, the pragmatic tendency of the seventeenth-century Dutch to engage in what one historian euphemistically calls "nefarious traffic,"[1] accomplished with as little publicity as possible, has obscured the full scope of Dutch activity.

Modern American archaeologists are finding the vestigial remains of this trade on numerous sites occupied or visited by the Dutch in the seventeenth century. Of these artifacts, ceramics are the most significant and the most helpful in interpreting both site chronology and economic and cultural implications of the Dutch trade. This is not because ceramics were a major item of the trade—they were not—but because progressive changes in their style of ornamentation or manufacture, as well as their resistance to the ravages of time and exposure to chemical elements in the soil, make ceramics one of the most useful and enduring tools for interpreting the past. Because of these peculiar qualities and the archaeological presence here of Dutch ceramics in large numbers, an understanding of these is invaluable to the archaeologist and necessary to the serious student of Dutch trade and settlement in America in the century of colonization.

Notes - Chapter 17

1. John Lothrop Motley, *History of the United Netherlands* (New York: Harper and Brothers, 1868), 3:545.

Bibliography

Aiello, Lucy L. "Burlington Island." *New Jersey History* 91 (1973): 24-34.

Albany Institute of History and Art, Albany, Manuscript FG807.

Andrews, Matthew Page. *Tercentenary History of Maryland.* 4 vols. Chicago: S. J. Clarke Publishing Co., 1925.

Aspinwall, William. *A Volume Relating to the Early History of Boston Containing the Aspinwall Notarial Records from 1644 to 1651* [*Aspinwall Papers*]. Boston: Municipal Printing Office, 1903.

Baart, Jan. "Ceramiche italiane rinvenute in Olanda e le prime imitazioni olandesi." In *Atti, XVI Convegno Internazionale della Ceramica* (Albisola, Italy, May 28-30, 1983). Albisola: Centro Ligure per la Storia della Ceramica, 1983.

——— . "Weserware in Amsterdam." In *Coppengrave—Studien zur Töpferei des 13. bis 19. Jahrhunderts in Nordwestdeutschland,* (by) Hans Georg Stephan. Hildescheim: 1981.

Bailyn, Bernard. *The New England Merchants in the Seventeenth Century.* New York: Harper and Row, 1964.

Bartlett, John R., ed. *Records of the Colony of Rhode Island and Providence Plantations, in New England, 1636-1663.* 10 vols. Providence: A. Crawford Greene and Brother, 1856-1865.

Beebe, Lucie B. "Rhenish Stoneware of the Renaissance." *American Ceramic Circle Bulletin,* 1980, no. 2: 125-40.

Bradford, William. *Bradford's History of Plymouth Plantation, 1606-1646.* Edited by William T. Davis. New York: Charles Scribner's Sons, 1908.

——— . *Letterbook.* In *Collections of the Massachusetts Historical Society for the Year 1794.* Vol. 3. Boston: 1810.

Bradley, James W. "Blue Crystals and Other Trinkets: Glass Beads from Sixteenth and Early Seventeenth Century New England." In *Proceedings of the 1982 Glass Trade Bead Conference,* Record 16. Rochester: Rochester Museum and Science Center, 1983.

Bradley, James W., and Monte Bennett. "Two Occurrences of Weser Slipware from Early Seventeenth Century Iroquois Sites in New York State." *Post-Medieval Archaeology* 18 (1984): 301-5.

Bridenbaugh, Carl. *Fat Mutton and Liberty of Conscience.* Providence: Brown University Press, 1974.

Browne, William Hand, ed. *Proceedings of the Council of Maryland, 1636-1667.* Baltimore: Maryland Historical Society, 1885.

Bruce, Philip A. *Economic History of Virginia in the Seventeenth Century.* 2 vols. New York: Macmillan and Co., 1896.

Caiger-Smith, Alan. *Tin-Glaze Pottery.* London: Faber and Faber, 1973.

Christensen, Aksel E. *Dutch Trade to the Baltic About 1600.* Copenhagen: Einar Munskgaard, 1941.

Cohen, Ronald D. "The Hartford Treaty of 1650." *New-York Historical Society Quarterly* 53 (1969): 311-32.

"Continental Post-Medieval Wares." *East Anglian Archaeology,* Report 13 (1981): 134-36.

Cox, Warren. *The Book of Pottery and Porcelain.* 2 vols. New York: Crown Publishers, 1946.

Craven, Wesley Frank. *Dissolution of the Virginia Company.* Gloucester, Mass.: Peter Smith, 1964.

Curtis, Julia B. "Chinese Ceramics and the Dutch Connection in Early Seventeenth Century Virginia." *Vereniging van vrienden der Aziatische kunst Amsterdam, Mededelingenblad* 15 (February 1985): 6-13.

De Jonge, Caroline H. *Delft Ceramics.* New York: Praeger, 1970.

——— . *Dutch Tiles.* Translated by P. S. Falla. New York: Praeger, 1971.

——— . *Oud-Nederlandsche majolica en Delftsch aardewerke, 1550-1800.* Amsterdam: Scheltema en Holkema, 1947.

Dictionary of American Biography.

Dutch Settlers Society of Albany. *Yearbook.*

Elzinga, G., and Dingeman Korf. *Vondsten uit eigen bodem.* Fries Museum Facetten 9. Leeuwarden: Fries Museum, 1978.

Encyclopaedia Britannica, 11th ed.

(F.W.B.) "Inter-Colony Trading." *de Halve Maen* 55 (Spring 1980): 21.

Fernow, Berthold. *Documents Relating to the History of the Dutch and Swedish Settlements on the Delaware River.* Albany: Argus Co., 1877.

——— . *Documents Relating to the History of the Early Colonial Settlements Principally on Long Island.* Albany: Weed, Parsons and Co., 1883.

Fourest, Henry-Pierre. *Delftware: Faience Production at Delft.* Translated by Katherine Watson. New York: Rizzoli, 1980.

Goggin, John M. *Spanish Majolica in the New World.* Yale University Publications in Archaeology, no. 72. New Haven: Yale University Press, 1968.

——— . *The Spanish Olive Jar: An Introductory Study.* Yale University Publications in Archaeology, no. 62. New Haven: Yale University Press, 1960.

Goodwin, William B. "Notes Regarding the Origin of Fort Ninigret in the Narragansett Country at Charlestown." *Rhode Island Historical Society Collections* 25 (January 1932): 1-16.

Green, Jeremy N., ed. *The Loss of the 'Verenidge Oostindische Compagnie Jacht Vergulde Draeck,' Western Australia, 1656.* BAR Supplementary Series 36, nos. 1 & 2. Oxford: 1977.

Grieve, Robert. "The Sea Trade and Its Development in Rhode Island and Providence Plantations." In *State of Rhode Island and Providence Plantations at the End of a Century*, 2 vols., edited by Edward Field. Boston: Mason Publishing Co., 1902.

Gronhagen, Juhani. "Underwater Archaeology in Finland." Paper read at meeting of the Society for Historical Archaeology, Boston, January 1985.

Hamilton, Alexander. *Itinerarium*. St. Louis: Bixby, 1907.

Havard, Henry. *Histoire de la faïence de Delft.* 2 vols. Paris: E. Plon et Cie., 1878.

Hayashiya, Seizo, and Henry Trubner. *Chinese Ceramics from Japanese Collections.* New York: Asia Society, 1977.

Heite, Edward F., and Louise B. Heite. "Report of Phase I Archaeological and Historical Investigation at the Site of Fort Casimir, New Castle, Delaware." Report prepared for Trustees of New Castle Commons, Delaware, September 1986.

Hobson, R. L. *Chinese Pottery and Porcelain.* 2 vols. 1915. Reprint (2 vols. in 1). New York: Dover Publications, 1976.

Holling, F. "Reflections on Tudor Green." *Post-Medieval Archaeology* 11 (1977): 61-63.

Hudig, Ferrand. "Wapengoet en porceleyn." *Oud Holland* 43 (1926): 162-81.

Huey, Paul R. "Archaeological Excavations in the Site of Fort Orange, a Dutch West India Company Trading Fort Built in 1624." *Bulletin, KNOB* (Royal Dutch Antiquarian Society) 84 (June 1985): 68-79

_____ . "Dutch Sites of the Seventeenth Century in Rensselaerswyck." In *The Scope of Historical Archaeology: Essays in Honor of John L. Cotter*, edited by David G. Orr and Daniel G. Crozier. Philadelphia: Temple University, 1984.

_____ . "Historical and Archaeological Research and Research Questions on Seventeenth Century Dutch New Netherland." Paper read at Colonial Dutch Symposium, New York University, March 2, 1985.

Hunt, George T. *The Wars of the Iroquois.* Madison: University of Wisconsin Press, 1940.

Hurst, John G. "Weser Slipware from Britain and North America." In *Coppengrave—Studien zur Töpferei des 13. bis 19. Jahrhunderts in Nordwestdeutschland*, (by) Hans Georg Stephan. Hildescheim: 1981.

Hurst, John G., D. S. Neal, and H. J. E. van Beuningen. "North Holland Slipware." In *Rotterdam Papers* 2. Rotterdam: J. G. N. Renaud, 1975.

Jameson, J. Franklin, ed. *Narratives of New Netherland, 1609-1664.* New York: Charles Scribner's Sons, 1909.

Johnson, Amandus. *The Swedish Settlements on the Delaware, 1638-1664.* 2 vols. Baltimore: Genealogical Publishing Co., 1969.

Kent, Barry C. *Susquehanna's Indians.* Harrisburg: Pennsylvania Historical Museum, 1984.

Kingsbury, Susan M., ed. *The Records of the Virginia Company of London.* 4 vols. Washington: Government Printing Office, 1906-1935.

Klesse, Brigitte. *Majolika.* Cologne: Kunstgewerbemuseum der Stadt, 1966.

Koetschau, Karl. *Rheinisches Steinzeug.* Munich: Kurt Woeff, 1924.

Korf, Dingeman. *Dutch Tiles.* New York: Universe Books, 1964.

_____ . *Nederlandse majolica.* 4th ed. Bussum: 1973.

_____ . *Nederlandse majolica.* 5th ed. Haarlem: De Haan, 1981.

Kukla, Jon. "Political Institutions in Virginia, 1619-1660." Thesis, University of Toronto, 1969.

Kupp, Jan. "Aspects of New York-Dutch Trade under the English, 1670-1674." *New-York Historical Society Quarterly* 58 (1974): 139-47.

_____ . "Dutch Notarial Acts Relating to the Tobacco Trade in Virginia." *William and Mary Quarterly* 80 (1973): 653-55.

McCrady, Edward. *History of South Carolina under the Proprietary Government, 1670-1719.* New York: Macmillan and Co., 1897.

Matson, Cathy. "Commerce after the Conquest: Dutch Traders and Goods in New York City." *de Halve Maen* 59 (4), forthcoming.

Mayflower Descendant 2 (July 1900): 155-57.

Miedema, Hessel. "Noordnederlandse majolica: kast opruimen." *Oud Holland* 97 (1983): 224-56.

Miller, Henry M. *A Search for the "Citty of Saint Maries."* St. Mary's City Archaeology Series, no. 1. St. Mary's City, Md.: St. Mary's City Commission, 1983.

Motley, John Lothrop. *History of the United Netherlands.* 4 vols. New York: Harper and Brothers, 1868.

Neill, Edward D. *History of the Virginia Company of London.* New York: Burt Franklin, 1968.

Neurdenburg, Elisabeth. *Old Dutch Pottery and Tiles.* Edited and translated by Bernard Rackham. New York: Himebaugh and Browne, 1923.

New York Historical Manuscripts: Dutch. Vols. 1, 2, 3, *Register of the Provincial Secretary of New Netherland [1638-1660].* Edited by Kenneth Scott and Kenn Stryker-Rodda, and translated by Arnold J. F. van Laer. Baltimore: Genealogical Publishing Co., 1974.

New York Historical Manuscripts: Dutch. Vol. 4, *Council Minutes, 1638-1649.* Edited by Kenneth Scott and Kenn Stryker-Rodda, and translated by Arnold J. F. van Laer. Baltimore: Genealogical Publishing Co., 1974.

New York Historical Manuscripts: Dutch. The Register of Salomon Lachaire, Notary Public at New Amsterdam, 1661-1662. Edited by Kenneth Scott and Kenn Stryker-Rodda, and translated by E. B. O'Callaghan. Baltimore: Genealogical Publishing Co., 1978.

New York Historical Manuscripts: Dutch. Vols. GG, HH & II, *Land Papers [1632-1664].* Edited and translated by Charles T. Gehring. Baltimore: Genealogical Publishing Co., 1980.

New York Historical Manuscripts: Dutch. Vol. 5, *Council Minutes, 1652-1654.* Edited and translated by Charles T. Gehring. Baltimore: Genealogical Publishing Co., 1983.

New York State Library, Albany. New York Colonial Manuscripts.

Noël Hume, Ivor. *All the Best Rubbish.* New York: Harper and Row, 1974.

_____ . *Early English Delftware from London and Virginia.* Colonial Williamsburg Occasional Papers in Archaeology, no. 2. Williamsburg: Colonial Williamsburg Foundation, 1977.

_____ . *A Guide to Artifacts of Colonial America.* New York: Alfred A. Knopf, 1970.

Northington, Oscar F., Jr. "The First Century of Virginia Tobacco." Thesis, College of William and Mary, 1929.

O'Callaghan, Edmund B. *Documents Relative to the Colonial History of the State of New York*. 14 vols. Albany: Weed, Parsons and Co., 1853-1858.

_____. *History of New Netherland*. 2 vols. New York: D. Appleton and Co., 1848.

Pagan, John R. "Dutch Maritime and Commercial Activity in Mid-Seventeenth Century Virginia." *Virginia Magazine of History and Biography* 90 (1982): 485-501.

Paxson, Henry D. *Sketch and Map of a Trip from Philadelphia to Tinicum Island, Delaware County, Pennsylvania*. Philadelphia: George H. Buchanan Co., 1926.

Philadelphia Museum of Art. *Dutch Tiles in the Philadelphia Museum of Art*. New Haven: Eastern Press, 1984.

Piccolpasso, Cipriano. *The Three Books of the Potter's Art*. Translated and with introduction by Bernard Rackham and Albert van der Put. London: Victoria and Albert Museum, 1934.

Pit, A. "Oude Noord-Nederlandsche majolica." *Oud Holland* 27 (1909): 133-41.

Public Records of Connecticut. Hartford: Brown and Parsons, 1850.

Rackham, Bernard. "Early Dutch Maiolica and Its English Kindred." *Burlington Magazine* 33 (1918): 116-23.

_____. *Early Netherlands Maiolica*. London: Geoffrey Bles, 1926.

Ray, Anthony. *English Delftware Pottery*. Boston: Boston Book and Art Shop, 1968.

Rink, Oliver. "New Netherland and the Amsterdam Merchants: Unraveling a Secret Colonialism." *de Halve Maen* 59 (4), forthcoming.

Ritchie, Robert C. "London Merchants, the New York Market, and the Recall of Sir Edmund Andros." *New York History* 57 (January 1976): 5-29.

Salwen, Bert, and Susan N. Mayer. "Indian Archaeology in Rhode Island." *Archaeology* 31 (1978): 57-58.

Sanford, Peleg. *The Letterbook of Peleg Sanford of Newport, Merchant, 1666-1668*. Providence: Rhode Island Historical Society, 1928.

Schuyler, George W. *Colonial New York*. 2 vols. New York: Charles Scribner's Sons, 1885.

Semmes, Raphael. *Captains and Mariners of Early Maryland*. Baltimore: Johns Hopkins Press, 1937.

Solis-Cohen, Lita. "Hatcher's China from the Sea." *Maine Antique Digest* (September 1984): 18B-21B.

Stanbury, Myra, comp. *Batavia Catalog*. Perth, Australia: Western Australian Museum, 1974.

Steiner, Bernard C. *Maryland Under the Commonwealth, 1649-1658*. Johns Hopkins University Studies, series 29, no. 1. Baltimore: Johns Hopkins Press, 1911.

Sturtevant, William C., ed. *Handbook of North American Indians*. Vol. 15. Edited by Bruce Trigger. Washington, D.C.: Smithsonian Institution, 1978.

Swanton, John R. *The Indian Tribes of North America*. Bureau of American Ethnology Bulletin, no. 145. Washington, D.C.: Smithsonian Institution, 1952.

Thijssen, J. R. A. M. "Gebruiksaardewerk met loodglazur." In *Van huisvuil tot museumstuk*. Nijmegen: Nijmeegs Museum Commanderie van Sint Jan, 1981.

Thwaite, Anthony. "The Chronology of the Bellarmine Jug." *Connoisseur* 182 (1973): 255-62.

Tietzel, Brigitte. *Fayence*. Cologne: Kunstgewerbemuseum der Stadt, 1980.

Trumbull, F. Hammond, ed. *The Public Records of the Colony of Connecticut*. 2 vols. Hartford: Brown and Parsons, 1850.

Valenstein, Suzanne G. *A Handbook of Chinese Ceramics*. New York: Metropolitan Museum of Art, 1975.

Van Beuningen, H. J. E. *Verdraaid goed gedraaid*. Rotterdam: Museum Boymans-van Beuningen, 1973.

Van Dam, J. D. "Geleyersgoet en Hollants porceleyn: Ontwikkelingen in de Nederlandse aardewerk-industrie, 1560-1660." *Mededelingenblad, Nederlandse vereniging van vrienden van de ceramiek* 108 (1982/84): 13-88.

Van der Pijl-Ketel, C. L., ed. *The Ceramic Load of the 'Witte Leeuw' (1613)*. Amsterdam: Rijksmuseum, n.d.

Van Laer, Arnold J. F., ed. and trans. *Documents Relating to New Netherland, 1624-1626*. San Marino, Calif.: Henry E. Huntington Library and Art Gallery, 1924.

_____, ed. and trans. *Van Rensselaer Bowier Manuscripts*. Albany: University of the State of New York, 1908.

Van Rensselaer, Jeremias. *Correspondence*. Edited and translated by Arnold J. F. van Laer. Albany: University of the State of New York, 1932.

Von Bock, Gisela Reineking. *Steinzeug*. Cologne: Kunstgewerbemuseum der Stadt, 1976.

Von Falke, Otto. *Das Rheinische Steinzeug*. 2 vols. Osnabrück: Otto Zeller, 1977.

Weeden, William B. *Economic and Social History of New England, 1620-1789*. 2 vols. New York: Hillary House Publishers, 1963.

Wertenbaker, Thomas J. *The Planters of Colonial Virginia*. New York: Russell and Russell, 1958.

Weslager, Clinton Alfred, in collaboration with Arthur Roy Dunlap. *Dutch Explorers, Traders and Settlers in the Delaware Valley, 1609-1664*. Philadelphia: University of Pennsylvania Press, 1961.

Whitehouse, David. "The Origins of Italian Maiolica." *Archaeology* 31 (1978): 42-49.

Wilcoxen, Charlotte. "Dutch Majolica of the Seventeenth Century." *American Ceramic Circle Bulletin*, 1982, no. 3: 17-28.

Winsor, Justin. *Memorial History of Boston*. 4 vols. Boston: James Osgood and Co., 1880.

_____. *Narrative and Critical History of America*. 8 vols. New York: AMS Press, 1967.

Winthrop, John. *Journal, 1630-1649*. 2 vols. Edited by James Kendall Hosmer. New York: Charles Scribner's Sons, 1908.

Wyckoff, Vertrees J. *Tobacco Regulation in Colonial Maryland*. Baltimore: Johns Hopkins Press, 1936.

Index

References to photographs are in italics

Dutch trade with, 23-25, 93
founding of, 23
proprietors of, 23
Marzacotto, 60
Mason, Captain John, 27
Massachusetts
ceramics found on sites in, 87
Massachusetts Bay colony
Dutch trade with, 35-37
legal code of, 27
Massachusetts Historical Commission, 13
Matinneconck, 90
Matson, Cathy, 47
Maverick, Samuel, 36
Mayer, Susan, 39
Medici, Francesco de', 67
Melyn, Cornelis, 40
Mereness, Newton D., 23
Mesopotamia, 57
Middelburg (Zeeland), 19, 58, 67
Miedema, Hessel, 64
Miller, Henry, 56
Ming dynasty. *See* China; Ming dynasty; Porcelain, Chinese: Ming
Minuit, Peter, 91
Mohawk River, 92
Motley, John, 13
Museum catalogs, 56, 69-70, 71
Museums, American
Dutch ceramics in, 79
Island Field Museum, 91
Philadelphia Museum of Art, 71
State Museum of Pennsylvania (Harrisburg), 92
University of Pennsylvania Museum (Philadelphia), 90, 91
Museums, British
Dutch majolica in, 79
London Museum, 79
Museums, Dutch
Frans Hals Museum (Haarlem), 70
Fries Museum (Leeuwarden), 56
Museum Boymans-van Beuningen (Rotterdam), 56
Nijmeegs Museum (Nijmegen), 56
Princessehof Museum (Leeuwarden), 54, 70
Rijksmuseum (Amsterdam), 77

Narragansett Bay area, 39, 41
Nassau, Duchy of (Germany), 73
Navigation Acts
defiance of, 16, 25, 46, 49
Dutch protest of, 21
effects of
on Dutch trade with Maryland, 24
on Dutch trade with Rhode Island, 41
historians' view of, 49
passage of, 15, 20
Navigation laws, British. *See also* Navigation Acts
defiance of, 13
effect on trade, 15
Netherlands, the. *See also names of individual towns*
early potteries in, 58
exploration and trade by, 13-17, 95
industrial progress of, 15
Italian potters in, 58
maritime superiority of, 15
wars with England, 16, 17n. 16, 59
Netzornament, 75, 75, 89
Netzwerk, 75
Neurdenburg, Elisabeth, 63

New Amstel, Del., 91
New Amsterdam, 89-90. *See also* New Netherland
New Castle, Del., 91, 92
New Castle Commons, 92
New England. *See also names of individual colonies*
Dutch trade with, 27-29
manufacturing in, 28
and New Netherland, boundary between, 32
overseas trade of, 29, 93n. 21
ship-building in, 29
shortage of money in, 28
New Gothenborg, 91
New Haven, Conn., 28, 43
New Jersey, 14
archaeological sites in, 90-92 (*see also names of individual sites*)
New Jersey Historical Society, 91
New Netherland
administration of, by Dutch West India Company, 14, 89
archaeological sites on former territory of, 81-92
English claims to, 31
English ownership of, 16
English takeover of, 39, 41, 45
founding as trading colony, 14
lack of material support for, 46
location of, 14, 39
manufacturing forbidden in, 28
patroon system of, 14
trade with other colonies, 14, 16 (*see also names of individual colonies*)
years of existence, 16
New Plymouth Company. *See* Plymouth Company
Newport, R.I., 41
New York
Dutch in, 45, 46, 47, 65
Dutch trade with, 45-47
restrictions on, 46
lack of material support for, 46
population of, 45
women of, 45
New York City. *See also* Manhattan
Dutch merchants of, 45, 47
as fur-trading center, 46
New York State Historic Trust, 82
New York State Office of Parks, Recreation and Historic Preservation, 82
Nicolls, Richard, 16, 46
Nijmegen (Gelderland), 56
Noël Hume, Ivor, 89
North Carolina, 49
North Holland, 55
Northington, Oscar F., Jr., 21

O'Callaghan, Edmund B., 31

Pagan, John R., 21
Paintings, Dutch *genre*, 53, 57, 57, 59
Pavonia, 92
Pennsylvania
archaeological sites in, 90-91 (*see also names of individual sites*)
Dutch trade with, 49
Pennsylvania Historical Society, 91
Philadelphia, 91
Piccolpasso, Cipriano, 57, 58, 60
Pickman, Arnold, 90
Pietersen, Abraham, 39
Pit, A., 63

About the Author

Charlotte Wilcoxen, Research Associate for the Albany Institute of History & Art, began her writing career as a newspaper reporter in Paducah, Kentucky. After moving north to Schenectady, New York, she began to collect ceramics amidst the trials and joys of rearing seven children. Finding her curiosity on early seventeenth-century ceramics only partially satisfied by the literature available in English, Mrs. Wilcoxen made the first of a series of research visits to the Netherlands in 1980, where she consulted directly with specialists in this field. Subsequently, she devoted time each week for five years to work with the New York State Office of Parks, Recreation and Historic Preservation in analyzing and processing sherds from early seventeenth-century Dutch settlement sites in New York State. During this intensive study she also visited archaeological sites in New England and Virginia to examine Dutch ceramic sherds found in these localities.

Mrs. Wilcoxen wrote another book, *Seventeenth Century Albany: A Dutch Profile*, which is now in its second edition (Albany Institute, 1981 & 1984). A concise, overall examination of the first century of settlement, this book corrected misinformation that began with nineteenth-century historians and was perpetuated by later writers. During the last twenty years, Mrs. Wilcoxen has written articles on seventeenth- and eighteenth-century ceramics, Albany silver and Indian trade silver for *Antiques Magazine, New-York Historical Society Quarterly, American Ceramic Circle Bulletin* and other publications. Mrs. Wilcoxen has lectured widely on her fields of interest. She frequently teaches Dutch ceramics classes designed for archaeologists and museum curators and researchers. In 1987, the New York State Library selected this energetic scholar for one of its first three Research Resident Awards.